MW01595178

Unlikely
Finding Faith in the Wilderness of Fear

By Jo Elaine Hooper

Unlikely: Finding Faith in the Wilderness of Fear
Copyright © 2019 by Jo Elaine Hooper
All Rights Reserved

No part of this book may be used, reproduced, uploaded, stored or introduced into a retrieval system, or transmitted in any way or by any means (including electronic, mechanical, recording, or otherwise), without the prior written permission of the publisher, with the exception of brief quotations for written reviews or articles. No copying, uploading, or distribution of this book via the Internet is permissible.

Scriptures marked AMP are taken from the AMPLIFIED BIBLE, Copyright © 1954, 1958, 1962, 1964, 1965, 1987 by the Lockman Foundation Used by permission.

Scriptures marked ESV are taken from the THE HOLY BIBLE, ENGLISH STANDARD VERSION ® Copyright © 2001 by Crossway, a publishing ministry of Good News Publishers. Used by permission.

Scriptures marked KJV are taken from the KING JAMES VERSION (KJV): KING JAMES VERSION, public domain.

Scriptures marked NASB are taken from the NEW AMERICAN STANDARD BIBLE ®, Copyright © 1960, 1962, 1963, 1968, 1971, 1972, 1973, 1975, 1977, 1995 by The Lockman Foundation. Used by permission.

Scriptures marked NKJV are taken from the NEW KING JAMES VERSION: Copyright © 1982 by Thomas Nelson, Inc. Used by permission. All rights reserved.

Scriptures marked NLT are taken from the HOLY BIBLE, NEW LIVING TRANSLATION: Copyright © 1996, 2004, 2007 by Tyndale House Foundation. Used by permission of Tyndale House Publishers, Inc., Carol Stream, Illinois 60188. All rights reserved. Used by permission.

Scriptures marked PHILLIPS are taken from The New Testament in Modern English by J.B Phillips copyright © 1960, 1972 J. B. Phillips. Administered by The Archbishops' Council of the Church of England. Used by permission.

Scripture quotations marked MSG are taken from *THE MESSAGE*, copyright © 1993, 2002, 2018 by Eugene H. Peterson. Used by permission of NavPress. All rights reserved. Represented by Tyndale House Publishers, Inc.

Table of Contents

Dedication

For my parents, you lived this story long before I wrote it.

For my family, you keep me humble and dreaming.

For my friends, you love loudly and I'm grateful.

When everything was hopeless, Abraham believed anyway, deciding to live not on the basis of what he saw he <u>couldn't</u> do but on what God said he <u>would</u> do.

Romans 4:17-18 (MSG)

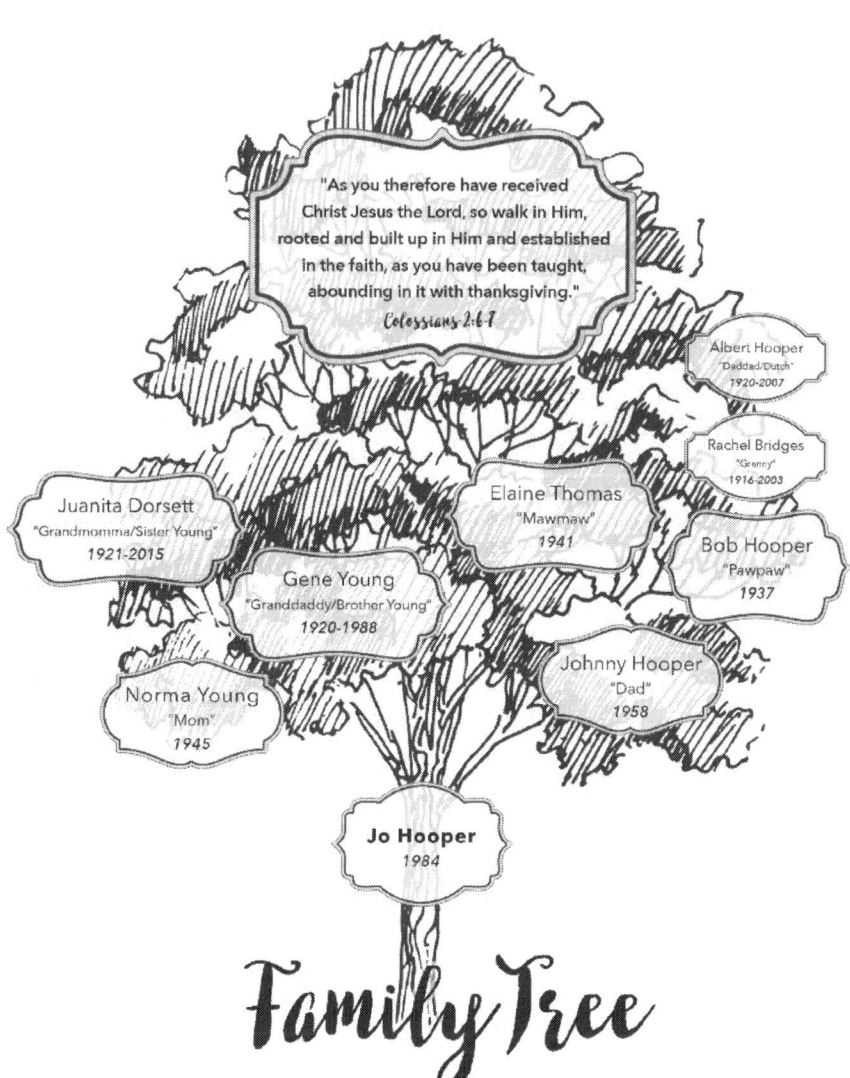

"As you therefore have received Christ Jesus the Lord, so walk in Him, rooted and built up in Him and established in the faith, as you have been taught, abounding in it with thanksgiving."
Colossians 2:6-7

Albert Hooper
"Daddad/Dutch"
1920-2007

Rachel Bridges
"Granny"
1916-2003

Juanita Dorsett
"Grandmomma/Sister Young"
1921-2015

Elaine Thomas
"Mawmaw"
1941

Bob Hooper
"Pawpaw"
1937

Gene Young
"Granddaddy/Brother Young"
1920-1988

Norma Young
"Mom"
1945

Johnny Hooper
"Dad"
1958

Jo Hooper
1984

Family Tree

Preface

It's often been said that the bumblebee shouldn't be able to fly. While science has proven that notion incorrect in recent years, there's still something sensational about that bee and his handiwork.

My father always told me that I was like that bee. Able. Artistic. Accomplished. Appreciated. But unlikely.

You see, no one told the bee that he was aerodynamically challenged. We spent almost a hundred years trying to explain the insect kingdom with airplane terminology, so that's how the myth became believable. The truth is that he just flies in unexpected ways. His wings beat more than two hundred and thirty times per second and in multiple directions, providing the lift and velocity he needs. He was designed by a magnificent Creator; he was born to fly whether we understand it or not. Just because it has been unexplainable does not make it untrue.

The same goes for me. The Lord has created me to do some special things. Dreaming, planning, writing, speaking, teaching, working – each are part of my divine assignment, the jobs I hold and the tasks I do. I am the unexpected messenger of an unbelievable story, simply your unlikely host. The Lord has entrusted me with this and while the circumstances cannot be entirely explained, I can guarantee it's 100% true.

This book began as a blog to commemorate the most difficult season of my life. The first five chapters detail exactly what my modern-day wilderness experience entailed, and the last ten chapters highlight everything we learned in those days and that we have learned in the many months since.

From where I stand, as a testament to the impossible, this is a pretty sweet spot. Just as it was for the children of Israel, the land on the other side of great heartache, pain and loss is worth it. There is a peace that only comes when you're asked to live past your level of understanding. There is a definition of prosperity that is only found after you've lost it all. There is a type of faith that is only developed by patience, persevering beyond all possibilities. For me and my family, that place is here, and that time is now. I'm living in my Canaan, a place of promise, the land still flowing with milk and honey.

PART I
Chapter One
Wounded

Most all stories have a beginning. When I first decided to write this memoir, I was tempted to start with my earliest memories. It was an average 1980's childhood in North Texas - nothing too extraordinary and fairly stereotypical. If we wanted to set the stage and go back even farther, I could begin with information that has only been told by the generations that have gone before me. Wouldn't you have loved to hear something like, "Once upon a time…" or "In a galaxy far, far away…"? We could start before 1900 and bring up everything from the Depression to the Dust Bowl. If you go back far enough, my family has seen it all.

Our story of faith has been written by more than seven generations; I'm just one role in a play with many moving parts. My life and the tale I get to tell are simply a screenshot, a very small piece of the whole. There's nothing spectacular about my story alone, but in context, our experiences are nothing short of astonishing.

I come from a long line of believers. Not just the Sunday school attenders, but the men and women who relied on Jesus to get them through each day. They raised families and buried babies; they prospered during seasons of plenty and survived during the even longer seasons of drought. The world was tough, but our faith was strong. In fact, I would dare to say that it's the one thing we pass on. For all the faults and failures, the faith of my father's still sustains us all.

That faith was only just developing when it had to withstand its first great trial. Like so many other Christ followers, we are no strangers to hard times. Call it persecution, call it tribulation, call it whatever you'd like; the reality is that trying circumstances are basically promised and unavoidable. My life and my faith have been tested more times than I care to recount, but it was in the first great wilderness that I found myself asking some of the world's biggest questions. Who am I? Why am I here? Why is this happening to me?

The whole experience, the years that have since followed and therefore the remainder of this book were the answer to all those questions. Every day provides another opportunity to trust and believe. Every decision must be faced with unwavering hope. Although I know the Scriptures and have followed Christ since my infancy, this was the time for truth and there has not been a moment since that this was untrue. I've tested these principles and I've unpacked every question and answer. Come to find out, faith is all that matters when you're wounded.

To Divulge Some Details

On June 21, 2005, my dad was helping my granddad set out grass in his backyard.

For the sake of the story, my dad's name is JB and we're always going to call my granddad Pawpaw. Now back to the story...

On June 21st, we knew it was hot but didn't think it was dangerous. These men have worked outdoors – in Texas – in the summer – for their entire lives. My dad knew to be careful and nothing should've been different about this day. With Pawpaw on the tractor and Dad on the ground, they were making great strides with this piece of dirt.

The process moved quickly, and they were finished before lunch. As was our norm, they called the rest of the family and we grabbed lunch together at a local Italian place. Everything was normal. Same seats, same drinks, same meals. Just another day in paradise.

After lunch, dad and Pawpaw headed over to their workshop to replace a radiator on our Suburban. It should've been fine. They were in the shade, in front of a fan, doing nothing too strenuous (or so we thought).

But that night, when we were out eating to celebrate my cousin's birthday, dad wanted to go home early. He's never been much for parties and crowds, so this was not yet an abnormal request. I gave him the car keys and he went home alone. During the night, he began throwing up. Unsure of what caused this and knowing that nothing had upset his stomach, he thought he could sleep it off.

He slept all day Wednesday, not being able to keep food or water down. When I tried to talk to him, his answers were mumbled. By that night, he wouldn't even try to talk or get out of bed. His mom came over first thing Thursday morning and we took him to the doctor. When they walked through the clinic doors, the doctor took one look at him and sent him straight to the emergency room.

When they checked his vitals, his blood pressure was 256/190. The doctors and nurses ran all their tests, medicated him and made him rest in the ER. In the late evening, they wanted to perform an MRI because the test results weren't making sense. Before they took him back, he was sitting in a wheelchair in the radiology waiting room. I asked him how things were going, and his only answer was that he still had the worst headache of his life. The fluids and medicine were helping, but he knew there was still something wrong.

After running the MRI, they asked him to stay overnight. Still dehydrated from being sick and still needing a few more doses of the blood pressure medicine to be given by IV, the hospital staff sent us home around 9 p.m., thinking we could come back and pick him up on Friday morning. That normal Friday morning never came.

I awoke at 2 a.m. to an unfamiliar voice leaving a message on the answering machine in my bedroom. It was a nurse saying that my dad was being sedated and that there had been some major complications. She assured me that there was no need to come to the hospital because visiting hours weren't for another four hours. Choosing to ignore that recommendation, I went to get my mom up. We called Pawpaw and Mawmaw and the four of us took two cars back to the hospital at 3 a.m. on June 24th.

The first doctor to see us explained the circumstances. Another MRI had revealed a golf-ball-sized brain bleed in my dad's right temporal lobe. There were two other small bleeds, but they didn't think those were causing a problem right now. The dye in the MRI had negatively interacted with my dad's dehydrated kidneys and he was experiencing kidney failure, respiratory arrest and cardiac shock. These sentences didn't process. We kept thinking, "What?" Even Pawpaw kept saying, "But he's going to be ok, right?"

The doctors decided to send my dad to a larger hospital, The Medical Center of Plano, since they would be better equipped for brain surgery. We followed the ambulance there and admitted him to the ICU at 8 a.m. on Friday morning.

This was the first time I had ever seen my grandparents cry. After the circumstances of that summer, we now express emotion differently and frequently discuss difficult situations. Until this event, we didn't typically discuss things that were too painful or too personal. Being people of faith, we always tried to be people of strength and resilience. On that bleak morning in June 2005 though, I had found something that shook us all to the core.

For Mawmaw and Pawpaw, when your forty-seven-year-old son may die at any time, you have the right to not be ok. For my mom, when you're looking at being a widow after only twenty-six years of marriage, you have a right to fall apart. For myself, when you're only twenty-years-old and facing the loss of the only man that ever loved you, you have a right to be forever changed.

Dad was the one laying in the hospital bed. Tubes running everywhere, ties holding his hands and feet, machines beeping and buzzing and dripping and drowning. But make no mistake, every single one of us was hurt that morning. We had all been wounded.

How we survived, I don't know. Some parts of that day are still a blur and I'm a little broken and tangled trying to remember it all even now. There has always been something about that day, whether it be in the surprise or the magnitude, that leaves me totally undone.

When we ran out of tears and words, I know God heard our silence.

Despite all the questions and pain, we had to experience that day, we found something new inside of ourselves that morning. The hope that was going to help us overcome had been inside of us all along. Seeds of Scripture planted decades earlier had found a reason to root. Prayers silently prayed but never understood had made their way to the throne. Intercession brought a peace we didn't know existed. When we ran out of tears and words, I know God heard our silence. We didn't know that the journey was just beginning, but we knew that from this point on, we were going to continue by faith alone.

Chapter Two
Wrecked

The first word that comes to mind is, "No." There's no way. This can't be happening to us. You must be talking about someone else. I can't believe everything I am seeing, hearing and feeling. No. Not me. Not us.

We were wrecked. Every plan, every idea, every task got shelved in a matter of moments. Settling in for what everyone said would be a long journey, there were many emotions we experienced before we become content in our waiting. We cried, and we prayed, and we sat, usually in silence. Numbness was the first feeling to find us. Grief made its way to that waiting room, making sure we knew life would never be the same. Loss was on the tip of our tongue, saying that this was life and death but not realizing how right we were. What once was easy and happy and free had quickly become dull and dry and dead. No words.

Trust Is a Choice

That day, I began to walk a new journey with Jesus. I've since been able to label it "Trust," but many of those closest to me know to call it "the T word." Even through the roughest times, our faith was unmovable. We could be startled and maybe even a little shaken, but asking us to renounce God or His goodness would not happen. I learned that I can accept anything by faith, and I can face horrible circumstances by knowing Jesus is by my side. But it wasn't until this summer that I learned I lacked trust.

Each time we spoke to the doctors, their news was the same. My dad had a golf-ball-sized brain bleed in his right temporal lobe.

What caused it? I don't know. When will it go away? I don't know. How will Dad be different? I don't know.

The neurosurgeons really wanted to do surgery to remove the buildup of pressure in Dad's brain, but one internist stopped them, believing surgery would likely kill him. With relatively no kidney function and major problems with both his heart and lungs, Dad wouldn't have been able to live through any of the planned procedures. Instead of jumping into action, that one doctor made them wait. She held them off for more than fourteen days, each time believing that waiting was best. We know she made a difficult choice, but we also know she was a Godsend.

While we navigated those first few days, I couldn't help but learn more about our situation. The primary function of your right temporal lobe is to communicate audio information and process that with other visual stimuli. That area of the brain was also responsible for long-term memory, language comprehension and personalities or behaviors. Dad's physical condition was considered barely stable, but there were many unknown variables we would be confronted with in the months and years to come because of this brain bleed.

As a preacher, my dad was self-taught. He doesn't have a theological degree, but he has a lifetime of Bible studying and experiences to rely upon. He put himself through school while driving a tractor, reading every book he could find and listening to hours' worth of teaching on cassette tapes. When the doctors mentioned long-term memory and language loss, we feared much of what Dad knew about the Bible would be affected. They tried to prepare us for his audio impairments, mentioning that he might not be able to speak or read. Everyone seemed to be most concerned with him even waking up; we had already begun to worry about playing music, singing and reading. After a few days of all the negativity piling up, I was forced to realize that their diagnosis was grim at best. I knew my father - and if he couldn't play, sing, teach, pray or be anything like his old self, then he was going to be even harder to live with than normal.

A Promise of Long Life

By Independence Day, we had been stuck at the hospital for more than a week. On July 4th, we were once again in Dad's ICU room after visiting hours. Our wonderful nurse had allowed us to stay. Her demeanor was so pleasant, and she was constantly checking on Dad, messing with machines, administering medicine, the whole deal. But when we didn't want to get up and leave, she said that was ok.

We tried to keep Dad's room dark and cold. The nurse had even found a floor fan and put it in the corner of his room to oscillate. So, with lights off and the sun down, it was a pretty dreamy place. Mom and I were standing by the windows, in front of Dad's fan, and we could see fireworks going off all over the city. We didn't feel like celebrating this year and everything was understandably a little more somber than usual. Sometimes, even the prettiest of pictures can't lift the darkest of moods.

When the fireworks display was over, we went to sit in two chairs by Dad's bed. As was her usual habit, Mom reached for the Bible on the table and placed it in her lap. She was reading to herself, but the nurse noticed and said we should read aloud. Praise the Lord for Bible-believing, God-fearing medical professionals! Medically, we still don't know much about a patient's comatose state, but the nurse assured us that talking to patients was very comforting and that she believed they knew what was going on.

Mom couldn't keep from crying to read aloud, so she handed me the Bible and pointed to the title of Psalm 91. Seldom has there been another sixteen verses that satisfied my soul like these.

He that dwelleth in the secret place of the Most High shall abide under the shadow of the Almighty.
I will say of the Lord, He is my refuge and my fortress: my God; in him will I trust.
Surely, he shall deliver thee from the snare of the fowler, and from the noisome pestilence.
He shall cover thee with his feathers, and under his wings shalt thou trust: his truth shall be thy shield and buckler.
Thou shalt not be afraid for the terror by night; nor for the arrow that flieth by day;
Nor for the pestilence that walketh in darkness; nor for the destruction that wasteth at noonday.
A thousand shall fall at thy side, and ten thousand at thy right hand; but it shall not come nigh thee.
Only with thine eyes shalt thou behold and see the reward of the wicked.

Because thou hast made the Lord, which is my refuge, even the most High, thy habitation;

There shall no evil befall thee, neither shall any plague come nigh thy dwelling.

For he shall give his angels charge over thee, to keep thee in all thy ways.

They shall bear thee up in their hands, lest thou dash thy foot against a stone.

Thou shalt tread upon the lion and adder: the young lion and the dragon shalt thou trample under feet.

Because he hath set his love upon me, therefore will I deliver him: I will set him on high, because he hath known my name.

He shall call upon me, and I will answer him: I will be with him in trouble; I will deliver him, and honour him.

With long life will I satisfy him and shew him my salvation.

Please forgive the King James translation, but it's what my heart knows best.

Standing by his hospital bed that night, I was able to read aloud until I saw verse 14. When the Lord says here, "I will set him on high, because he hath known my name," my walls fall apart and the tears rain down. There is no greater promise throughout all of Scripture. This invitation – to know and be known by God – changes everything.

These verses play back in my mind all the time. With any trial we face, in any hardship too big, this is what my spirit says. Just look at all the promises!

- I can abide with God; He will be my refuge and my fortress.
- I can trust Him; He will deliver me.
- I have nothing to fear – seen or unseen, big or small; He will be my habitation.
- I will not fall or fail; He will bear me up and set His love upon me.
- I will be satisfied with long life; He will hear me, answer me and show me His salvation.

It's this kind of intimacy that brings me to my knees in prayer. It's this level of care and attention that breaks my heart in the most tender of ways. The promise at the end of verse 15 is that those who know God and who call on Him will be honored. They will be satisfied with long life... and so begins the ugly cry. Long life. That was something I knew we needed right then and there. The other stuff was pretty. The other verses comforted and healed in some way, but I could shout LONG LIFE from the rooftops that night.

This invitation, to know and be known by God, changes everything.

Sometimes Scripture sounds good; other times it feels good. But in times like these, it is hope-sustaining, life-giving goodness flowing directly from the throne of God. Jesus knew what we needed to remember on this day. So, with everyone celebrating their independence outdoors, we were celebrating a new kind of dependence in the hospital room. The kind of reliance that only comes through loss, the ability to lose yourself in the plan of God and trust that He knows best and will only do good. That's what Psalm 91 is to me; it's a picture of life in the hands of my Creator. Dad's condition didn't change that night, but my opinions did. And now anytime I'm in a cold, dark room or a cold, dark situation, my heart knows where to turn, my eyes see His salvation and my soul rests in His wings.

Potentially Salvageable

What kind of person can hear bad news day after day and remain positive about their future? If you find someone with this ability, please have them call me so we can chat. In the middle of my wilderness, no matter how much faith we had, we were forced to face reality every day. Reality was not pretty, and we felt very wrecked by our circumstances. Isn't every difficult thing like that though? Just when you need to be upbeat all the time, circumstances make that next to impossible.

But I have a God that's into the difficult things.

I must believe that nothing is impossible for God. When I go back and read the Word, I love the parts about the underdog overcoming insane odds to win in the end. There are stories of giants and lions, opponents, armies, captives and an enemy. In the Bible, if anything was established, you can bet they had to face opposition. Believers have not historically been strong because their lives were easy; their strength came from finding courage despite it all. They were brave because they had to be. God's in the business of healing and mending, because the people He loves are broken and scarred.

In early July 2005, about eighteen days after our journey through this wilderness began, Dad's neurosurgeon called. Actually, he was calling me back. We never left the waiting room, but the doctors never came out there to see us. I had called them wanting an explanation about my dad's condition. The nurses had been as patient as possible with my questions, but they couldn't tell me what the doctor could. They forwarded my contact info onto him and he called late one afternoon. His bedside manner left much to be desired; come to find out, this is a common thing in the neuro field. He really didn't think I should be bothering him. I figured that we were paying the doctors and hospitals about $13,000 each day. He could take five minutes to chat with me.

He was willing to answer a few questions, but the one thing I needed to know, he never addressed. Finally, right before hanging up, I asked what the future would look like. That question plagued us every day, "Are we ever gonna get out of here? Will he ever wake up again?"

Very matter of factly, this doctor told me that my dad was potentially salvageable. His actual diagnosis of my father's condition sounded like something being barked from the foreman of a ship wrecking yard. "Yeah, that one there. He's potentially salvageable."

I still hear those words ringing in my ears; how in many ways, his statement was a non-statement. He didn't know how this would end. No one did. The one answer I wanted, I would never receive. I could show up every day. I could live by faith. I could do all the things right, trying to earn or deserve my answers. I could hope for the best, but I had to take what I was going to get. My life and my future were no longer in my own hands. How in the world could I make it better by myself? If I had truly surrendered to Jesus and His plan, then I was going to have to trust Him with this too.

I began to say the words "potentially salvageable" in my prayers every day. Not knowing what they meant or how I was supposed to take them, I took them to Jesus. He was going to have to help my unbelief. When conditions worsen, and problems persist, prayer is the only thing that can guarantee a change. Sometimes, we don't receive the answer we expect. Many times, our heart changes before our circumstances do. And this time was no different.

As I took this problem to God repeatedly, I'd carry a bit less of the burden each time. He began to take on my concern and my fear. God has not given us a promise and left us to wait alone. We might know that God doesn't forsake us, but also need to start believing that His presence is enough. His presence can't help but change things. It's not always in big ways and it's not always what I initially desired, but His presence is enough because it's all we need. In the wilderness, I didn't need to get my way. I didn't need all the answers. I didn't need for Him to fix it immediately. All I needed then and all I really need now is Him.

This is the perfect time to remind everyone that God will always be in the business of salvaging the useless and broken and hurting. The unlikely, the lost, dying, scared and alone. Dad being potentially salvageable to a doctor was a negative and uncertain thing, but to the Lord – the story had only begun. When I had lost all hope and when I thought I had nothing else to cling to, God had gone to work.

I managed my wreckage by diving deep into Scripture and finding some promises to hold onto. Almost every book of the Bible is filled with situations we can relate to. Instilling the idea that God can work on your behalf will be something that helps you sleep at night. You can rest as He constructs and destructs as necessary. He will build you something beautiful and worthwhile. He can be trusted and relied upon to complete all the work He's begun.

When everyone fails you, when bad news upsets you, when you see no way out and wonder if you'll ever make it through – these are not the times that God shies away. He is not deaf nor blind; He is not distant and cold. He is faithful and good – and His being near and His being good will always be enough.

Chapter Three
Waiting

I've never been the type of girl to love shopping. I enjoy wandering the air-conditioned stores for some alone time more than spending money, hunting for items or trying on clothes. But in the hospital, there was something comforting about the gift shop.

Friends would come to visit, and they'd bring us cards, flowers, balloons, books and snacks from the gift shop. When we needed to stretch our legs, our walk would inevitably end up there. We needed to see a different view and kill time. There weren't many places to roam, so we'd find ourselves looking at shelves full of things we didn't need or couldn't use. That was until I found a treasure I still see almost daily, a red leather bookmark that says:

Faith sees the invisible, believes the incredible and receives the impossible.

I'd place this in whatever book I was reading at the time, running my fingers through the tassels or over the stamped impressions of each word. This was something tangible that helped hold my faith together. The bookmark is lying here beside me as I type these words. It's been a perpetual reminder for many years now that God did exactly what He promised. The words may take me back to the sights, smells and sounds of our hospital time but this sentence means something deeper now. When my faith is at its lowest, little things like this bookmark remind me that I've already been carried through tougher times.

While in the middle of our crisis, I knew that I needed to receive something incredible. I wasn't sure if what we had asked was impossible. Believing someone could come back from being so close to death can be a tough, politically-incorrect subject. The doctors had grim news each time we spoke. With brain trauma, there is more uncertainty than you can prepare for. Without knowing all the statistics, it's fair to say that if Dad being healed wasn't impossible, then it was at least incredible.

When we are waiting on God's plan to take shape, we must stand on promises that might still be far away. I still face hard times, aiming to become more like Jesus isn't for the faint of heart. Even now, the words from my old, cheap bookmark stick with me. My faith has seen invisible things before. My faith has believed incredible truths. My faith has received what others would deem impossible. I've seen too much to turn back now.

This Sickness Is Not Unto Death

It's funny how I don't remember worrying in hindsight. A whole host of other emotions and thoughts come to mind when I reminisce, but worry is not something that stuck with me. Pieces of our hospital experience are such a blur while other parts remain intensely branded in my brain. I totally relate to these words found in the Old Testament.

Though the fig tree does not blossom and there is no fruit on the vines, [though] the product of the olive fails, and the fields yield no food, though the flock is cut off from the fold and there are no cattle in the stalls, Yet I will rejoice in the Lord; I will exult in the [victorious] God of my salvation! The Lord God is

my Strength, my personal bravery, and my invincible army; He makes my feet like hinds' feet and will make me to walk [not to stand still in terror, but to walk] and make [spiritual] progress upon my high places [of trouble, suffering, or responsibility]!
Habakkuk 3:17-19 (AMP)

Faith professes things that it cannot fathom, knows things that no one else understands and withstands more than we can handle alone.

I have come to know the God described in verse 19 above. I can experience God as my personal bravery and my invincible army. Sometimes I need that kind of ally. I need to know that I'm not hoping in the nonexistent and unknown. The Person I am waiting on is alive and real and powerful and careful and true.

Realizing this truth can create a crisis of faith if we're not careful. Like the verses say, we must praise and rejoice despite everything we see. Faith professes things that it can't fathom. Faith knows things that no one else understands. Faith withstands more than we can handle alone.

There is nothing I can't face with Jesus, but I also believe that I don't know how to face anything without Him. If I am walking and surviving, it is His strength in me. If I'm shining brightly in darkness, it's His light and love in me. If I am rejoicing in tribulation and watching my hope produce fruit, then that's Him too. Everything in my life can be boiled down to more of Him and less of me.

During the summer of the hospital wilderness, my mom and Mawmaw held a vigil in the waiting room. For the first two weeks, they didn't leave for any measurable amount of time. But somewhere in our third week, around day twenty, my mom came home. She still spent all her daylight hours at the hospital, but she decided she would start sleeping at home again.

In all her prayers and petitions, she had found enough peace to change her perspective. We believed everything the Bible said, but you can only sit by a hospital bed so long before you begin to get concerned. I don't consider confusion doubt, but it's weighty enough to impact your life. Instead of allowing our concern to become fear, we kept bringing our attention back to the Word. We were clinging to God like He was our only option – our lifeline, our consciousness and our plan. I can admit that I didn't have a plan B. If trusting Him didn't work out, then I don't know where I'd be. That's not faith or fear, just truth.

On the day that Mom came home, she would tell you that nothing physically changed, and the doctors were still set on being very negative and/or realistic. But we knew another option. Our faith did not overlook or deny our circumstances, but we choose to see other outcomes. Our faith knew that we could receive help and hope and health when no one else saw that as an option. Our God loves to operate in the impossible, so every bad day I've ever had is an opportunity to see Him at work.

We had been reading the Scriptures a lot each day, but we spent some time meditating on John 11:1-4. We would read it and think on it; we'd pray and ponder. When it finally sank in, these are the words we knew best:

> *A man named Lazarus was sick. He lived in Bethany with his sisters, Mary and Martha. This is the Mary who later poured the expensive perfume on the Lord's feet and wiped them with her hair. Her brother, Lazarus, was sick. So, the two sisters sent a message to Jesus telling him, "Lord, your dear friend is very sick." But when Jesus heard about it he said, "Lazarus's sickness will not end in death. No, it happened for the glory of God so that the Son of God will receive glory from this.*

When Jesus was walking on this earth, He made no mistakes. He was never in a hurry, never in the wrong place or with the wrong people. I believe that everything recorded in Scripture is for our benefit. There's something about this story that is meant to forever change the way I relate to God.

Here, Jesus is informed that Lazarus is sick. Lazarus, Mary and Martha were close to Christ, dear friends for what we believe had been many years. After hearing the bad news, Jesus continued teaching the crowds for two more days. His response to the news reveals a lot about God's purposes. Jesus didn't respond immediately for a divine reason – not because He didn't hear, not because He was unable, not because He didn't care. His response was perfect and sovereign. Hard to understand? Frustrating? Crazy at times? Yes, yes and yes. But despite the travel times and delayed communication, Jesus' response was still exactly what the situation needed.

When I invite Jesus into my circumstances, I must learn to rely on the same faith that has safely held so many others. I can confidently stand and wait and serve in the face of devastation because my God is good. The intensity of that summer in the hospital can only be matched by the brilliance of God. He made all things whole and new, even if I haven't yet seen the conclusion or purpose of every piece.

When He spoke life into existence and when we began to walk with Him, He declared that all the promises in the Bible would be mine. I can't always discern everything, and I don't always accept His ideas as best, but that never negates their perfection. Right on time, right where He belongs. When He said that sickness would not be unto death and that He would gain glory from even this, I cannot reason it away. I cannot doubt or fear or faint. I start looking for signs of life in a barren place. I start calling the wind and watching the bones. He will prove faithful and He will receive all my attention and if there is any glory to gain, it's His.

Timing Is Everything

Not receiving an answer to our prayers is a painful but unavoidable part of the human spiritual experience. Only partly seeing God's plan has strained my ability to relax and go with the flow. I'm a very controlling person, so asking me to take life as it comes is unnatural. I'm very prone to half-listen to an instruction and then mutter the words, "Thanks, I've got it from here." Sometimes, this works in my favor, but I've seen many more occasions where my exuberance was misplaced, and I messed things up. Hurry can hinder God's plan and devastate a destiny.

Hurry can hinder God's plan and devastate a destiny.

During our summer in the hospital wilderness, I learned (in more ways than one) how vital God's perfect plan is. You see, God has a purpose for my life. He also has a plan I am to follow. Now, this is normally where I screw things up. I want to take these two ideas and run with whatever makes me comfortable. If I'm capable of it and the idea makes logical sense, then that must be the plan of God! I'd rather be working than waiting. But the missing component is God's way. He wants to control both the big picture and the minute details. Nothing is out of His realm of care, and if I am to walk in His best, I must wait for His way.

It is possible to find, follow and fulfill God's will. God isn't requiring perfection from us, but He makes it possible. We cannot achieve all He has for our lives alone, but He makes even the most unimaginable thing conceivable. Just as the seed can bring forth a thirty-, sixty- or one hundred-fold return; we too can produce different harvests. It is my belief that the invitation and opportunity is always there. All the seeds sown in our life can produce enormous yield, but the ground must do its part. Only a life surrendered can meet its full potential. Only in the hands of its Creator does my heart know what to do.

There isn't anything sacred about my opinions in the grand scheme of life. I have ideas, and many of them I am passionate about. If you'd like to argue with me at any time, please just insinuate that I might not be right. I love to be right; it's the nastiest part of my personality. But in my relationship with God, my desire to be right robs me of Him. He can only do so much if I insist on having the final say, or of trying to add my two-cents to His perfect will. Especially in the quiet seasons of waiting, my mind races and my heart trembles in the presence of the unknown.

I feel that I've bargained with God often, and some of my greatest hang-ups come from this looming expectation of disappointment. Some things I want most in this life may not be a part of God's plan for me. Instead of surrendering fully to His ideas, I keep holding onto my selfish desires, hoping they are His too. Frankly, feeling let down is the likely outcome in these areas because I've prioritized my ability to control things over God's ability to work in my life. My behaviors belittle my beliefs. I have my opinions and ideas, and while God may like some of them and they might be rooted in things He's said, if I'm trying to build it on my own, then it will be without His blessing. It will also probably be incomplete and not substantial enough to survive what I cannot foresee.

That's the biggest blessing of having God be in control. He knows and sees everything. Anything He orchestrates and directs reaches farther and lasts longer than you could humanly expect. He takes nothing for granted and wastes no time or space. If some good can be brought to a situation, you can bet it's going to be because I've allowed God total access to my future, present and past.

While we were sitting in the waiting room, time dragged on at an excruciatingly slow pace. Minutes seemed like hours and the days felt like months. Even for Dad, if you said he was in a coma for ten years, he would've believed you. And if I had been in control of the whole situation, I'd like to say that I would've avoided the hospital wilderness altogether. Yeah, right. Let's be honest. If I had been in control of my life from the start, we wouldn't have even made it to 2005!

When the waiting was the hardest, I never asked God to hurry up. When He was all I had to wait on and I was truly answerless, I had no problem relinquishing control. There was no bargaining, no earning, no exchange. It was me, curled up in a crying ball on the bathroom floor, asking God to so overwhelm my heart so I could heal. If I was going to survive, it was going to be because of Him.

Oh, how quickly we can forget.

When life was rebuilt, and everyone was healthy again, I felt that self-sustaining lie creep back into my heart, that useless idea that I could possibly do something on my own and that my ways would be better than His. I'll tell you right now, it takes just as much faith to give God your good days as it does to give Him your bad ones. True surrender is allowing God to be in control and following Him at full speed when you would be capable to taking the reins yourself.

That's where I stand today. Life is good and getting better all the time. I still approach situations with my preconceived notions and I still have my own ideas that I'd like Jesus to fulfill. But now, because I can remember waiting in the wilderness, I'm more at ease with asking Him to see me through. God is still sovereign, even if I don't understand. He is still trustworthy, even when I am weary of waiting. It's a dangerous game to play, if we think we can both submit and control our destiny. The only safe bet is to give everything over and go along for the ride. Every decision will be vetted by the only Person that truly knows what's best. Every circumstance will prepare us for what lies ahead, and even the bad, scary, unforeseen outcomes will be used for your good and God's glory.

> *For the vision is yet for the appointed time; It hastens toward the goal and it will not fail. Though it tarries, wait for it; For it will certainly come, it will not delay.*
>
> *Habakkuk 2:3 (NASB)*

Ultimately, I find total surrender to be the hardest part of faith. He is so faithful, even when I am faithless, so trustworthy to a people who can't even spell that word. If I can earn God's grace or help Him accomplish His will in some way, then I can feel like I am in control. But the facade only resembles control; I have no real power once I have fully sought the Lord.

Anything that involves faith is going to be a struggle that is worth it all. Don't expect it to be fast, cheap or easy. I'm not even sure we'll ever get better at it. People still hurt us; situations will still stun and surprise. But the one thing we must never be shocked by is God's presence and power... and how important they can be in our lives. Having only half of God's will is not enough to see us through. We must continue to hold out for His perfect will, only then can we be complete and whole and blessed.

First-Hand Faith

I know from first-hand experience that waiting is going to be required. No matter what your past, present or future looks like, waiting will be a part of your story. In the moments when you have no answers and the pain is more than you can bear, what do you know to be true first-hand? How has your faith been tested and tried, stretched, pulled or purified?

That which was from the beginning, which we have heard, which we have seen with our eyes, which we have looked upon, and our hands have handled, of the Word of life; (For the life was manifested, and we have seen it, and bear witness, and shew unto you that eternal life, which was with the Father, and was manifested unto us;) That which we have seen and heard declare we unto you, that ye also may have fellowship with us: and truly our fellowship is with the Father, and with his Son

Jesus Christ. And these things write we unto you, that your joy may be full.

1 John 1:1-4 (KJV)

The apostle John was encouraging the church with his testimony and everything he had learned from walking with Jesus. He had heard, seen and handled the Son of God. Nothing was going to convince him to renounce his faith. Death threats couldn't deter him. Politicians couldn't silence him. Social expectations couldn't keep him bound. When you've seen something undeniable and you're forever changed by the Lord Himself, there's nothing that can move you. Shake? Stress? Concern? Yes. But not move. There is a type of relationship with God that you would be willing to give your life for. The Gospel, our souls and eternity are serious matters, whether we treat them that way or not.

Faith redeems tribulation with a testimony and God will want to use that testimony all the time. Being willing to tell all these stories was hard; it took God more than ten years to prepare me and give me the words to share. My heart knows that Jesus is waiting to do something miraculous; I believe He's begging me to believe. It may not always come where and when or in the ways I expected, but I've yet to see Him disappoint.

My faith wavered and weakened while I waited in the wilderness of a hospital room; it's hard to keep the faith when all you hear is bad news and sad tales. So, on the day my walk to the gift shop ended with the frivolous purchase of a red leather bookmark, something changed. Those words healed me then and they inspire me now. We will see, believe and receive out of a faithful expectation in the most Faithful One. We have strong days and we still see our fair share of tough stuff, but we cannot be moved. And boy, I hope we have a few more stories to tell.

Chapter Four
Wrestling

It's common to run through our lives each day, giving little thought to how fragile we are. I have found that people who survive life and death situations usually have a better grasp of that. When you have dreams and plans for tomorrow and then are suddenly awakened to the reality that tomorrow may never come, you learn lessons and struggle with concepts most other people never entertain.

Truth is, we do not have plenty of time.

It's cliché to say that we are not promised our next breath, but I've seen it to be true. I've been told that everything would be ok, only to receive phone calls proving otherwise. I've sat by families grieving the loss of a young loved one, bright lights gone long before their time. I've administered CPR to a person everyone would've deemed healthy and in their prime. I've been shaken by car accidents, natural disasters, bothers and burdens that I could've never foreseen and that no one would've ever planned for. The fact that we have this one chance at life weighs heavily on my mind.

A whole generation has chosen YOLO as their cry. In long form, that's "You Only Live Once." It's a true statement, but far from the whole story. We have each been graced with gifts and talents, but we only have a limited amount of time to impact the world. We are not infinite. We are also not invincible. Each small increment of time matters. God has not made any mistakes. We belong here. This time, this place, this season, these opportunities - all are a part of God's divine plan and purpose.

When you start talking about life in terms of limits, our priorities should become clear. No one is guaranteed time, but every day holds the potential for us to make the world a better place. Let's keep combining those two ideas:

every moment matters

+

time is not guaranteed

=

every small moment is more than special, it's sacred.

For twenty-eight days, we sat in a hospital waiting room simply trying to survive. When our life was put on hold during Dad's hospital stay, we all had to begrudgingly admit that his life may stop right there. It's a scary proposition, but was his story over? No edits. No amendments. No fixes. No intentions or explanations. Could we live with what was?

Time is a precious commodity, totally out of our control and still totally under our authority. My family is as guilty as anyone else when it comes to acting like we have all the time in the world. Some of us procrastinate. We over-commit and under-produce, always thinking that there will be time to fix it or just do better next time. We are too busy. At times, we're inefficient. Time may be

Time is a precious commodity, totally out of our control and still totally under our authority.

subjective, but it's also free. What am I to do with the time that has been entrusted into my hands?

See then that you walk circumspectly, not as fools but as wise, redeeming the time, because the days are evil. Therefore, do not be unwise, but understand what the will of the Lord is.

Ephesians 5:15-17 (NKJV)

On July 21, 2005, my dad woke up out of his coma. We had seen this through. Being told of his wounds, dealing with the wreckage and wallowing in the wait… we finally saw the outcome we had been hoping for. I hadn't yet thought about what the next few days, weeks, months and years might require. We didn't know to ask some of those long-term questions at the time. Our faith had taken up for us and God had seen us through. We would now wrestle with what was to come.

May the Lord Answer Your Cry

When I envision the life of David, I always focus on the years he reigned as king. I forget all his pain and the uncertainties he had to face. I overlook how lost he must have felt while waiting on God's promises to be fulfilled. David was fully human, struggling and stumbling through life but remaining faithful to God. Even when he became king and it appeared that all of God's plans were complete, David would remember God's goodness and the times he was afraid. He didn't forget, and he never only told half the story.

In times of trouble, may the LORD answer your cry. May the name of the God of Jacob keep you safe from all harm. May he send you help from his sanctuary and strengthen you from Jerusalem. May he remember all your gifts and look favorably on your burnt offerings. May he grant your heart's desires and make all your plans succeed. May we shout for joy when we hear of your victory and raise a victory banner in the name of our God. May the LORD answer all your prayers.

Psalm 20:1-6 (NLT)

The psalms are an accurate representation of David's walk. From one verse to the next, he ebbs and flows, from doubt and fear to praise and peace. It wasn't a yearly or weekly battle for him; just like for me, it was a moment-by-moment choice about whether to trust God.

David was unafraid to petition the throne of God with his problems. He was unconcerned about what others thought. Some might call it neediness, but I'm in awe of his ability to turn to God at a moment's notice. Like the psalm above reveals, David believed the Lord would answer an honest cry. He believed that the Lord searched for men and women to use, that He desired to intervene in the affairs of the world and that He needed willing vessels to do that work. Just by a simple petition and a willingness to see God move, David created a life marked by the plan and promises of God. Throughout David's story, God was his first choice, his last hope, his divine help, and his only answer.

During the summer of my wilderness experience, when my life was thrown into a state of sheer chaos, I found that Jesus was my only answer too. In the numerous situations that have tried to rattle me since, He is the only place worth turning to. When my lack was the problem, Jesus was the answer. When my pain was the problem, Jesus was the answer. When my doubt was the problem, Jesus was the answer. Keep going. When someone else's words were the problem, Jesus was the answer. When someone else's actions were the problem, Jesus was the answer. When my life had absolutely no certainty at all, there was Jesus and He was the answer.

And You Thought Waiting Was Hard?

Awakening from the coma became the middle of our story. What I thought would be the conclusion, the end result we had all been praying for, was in fact more like the climax at the end of Act II. Dad would spend two more days in ICU, followed by three days in a neurological unit. I didn't know at the time, but wrestling was harder than waiting.

Dad didn't remember getting sick, being sick or any of the events that led him here. All the medications were interacting with each other and his grasp of reality was loose at best. He didn't sleep well but was yet exhausted all the time. He had lost more than forty pounds in those twenty-eight days, so his muscle mass and memory had greatly deteriorated. He thought he was fine, but his own arms, legs and feet betrayed him. Not usually willing to accept help and never being a very good patient made for some very long days and excruciatingly long nights.

I was at a place in my life that ignoring this new reality would be easiest. Hang out with new friends, go to college classes, leave everyone else to sort it out – man, that was tempting! I had never had the desire to run away, but hiding was a naturally inviting escape during this season. Dealing with this new reality was not my favorite option, but it was the only right choice. It was time to hunker down and walk through the wilderness with the same faith that had led me this far along.

Someone recently reminded me that time heals all wounds. Y'all, I've tried to let time take her course and all I've ended up with is PTSD. I've found that time does nothing but either fester the pain or create a scar too deep to ever be fully healed. My God is not involved to see any of my pains or sufferings scab over; He is in this for reconciliation and restoration. He likes to see things be made new, even birthed again from the inside out. If I was waiting for time to help me move on, I'd be waiting forever. But I'm waiting on and wrestling with the Lord. He is attentive and swift, and His ways are perfect. Time is involved because that's how I measure life. Actions are involved because that's how I play my part. But my time and my actions alone will never heal me, and they will never bring about my life's fullest potential.

You see, a life fully surrendered to God has endless possibilities. In Psalm 20:4, David wishes that God would grant all our desires and make all our plans succeed. David's lament proves that victory is possible, that there can be things we need to be delivered from but that there are also countless moments we need to remember and give thanks for. On life's hard days, I have a difficult time accepting that God is with me and trying to make all my plans succeed. When everything falls apart and I'm left with the pieces of my plans, I don't understand. The best way I've found to cope is to try and absorb this one truth: my possibilities are limitless, but my vision is shortsighted.

I don't see the whole picture, so I don't know my best course of action. It's not me that has fallen short; I haven't failed. Sometimes, bad things happen, and I must wait and it's not my fault. Time doesn't make it better or worse. There's nothing I could've done to save some of the heartache I've experienced and there's no reason I need to skip through the difficult parts of my story. Avoiding conflict is comfortable, but it's unrealistic and can only produce a weak and flat character. In good times and in bad, I must remember that Jesus is still the answer. There's absolutely no circumstance I could dream up that He wouldn't be the answer for. He is still listening to my every cry, and He is moving as quickly as He can.

Knowing that God's presence should be answer enough, I no longer fear that I won't measure up. See, the psalmist asks the Lord to answer. David was living at a time when only the first half of God's story had been written. He still needed the hand of the Lord to move in miraculous and mighty ways. His reign over Israel started almost a thousand years before Jesus was born, so He didn't have a full Bible and a Spirit-filled option. I do. I'm on the downhill side of things, living life through the lens of the Gospel. God answered every question I could ever ask with one grace-filled act. David's psalms are encouraging, but I get to fully see how Jesus is God's answer to anything I face.

I believe God has a lot of stuff left for my family to finish. I know that we were very focused on what we could do for Jesus after Dad woke up. It's wonderfully common to analyze the how's and why's of being saved. We wanted to believe that we had been preserved for a purpose and we wanted to do God's gift justice. But I can also admit that it is still very easy to get comfortable and tired and distracted. When does seeking becoming striving? Just like when Jacob wrestled with God in Genesis 32, the story continues. The challenge is a vital part of who and what we are becoming, but it's not the end. We are now walking; we are weary but well.

Chapter Five
Walking

The wounds that wrecked us and left us waiting and wrestling with God's plan were now the very things that were allowing us to walk out of a rehab center, in the Word and on the mend. By the time we saw Dad wake up, we were spiritually and emotionally prepared for the breakthrough we were receiving. God had not given us a promise and then left us to wait alone; He was very present and doing a mighty work during the struggles and loss. He used every day of our experience. Every person that visited, every nurse that cared, everything that occurred. It was all for His glory, for His purpose, and not one piece was out of place. As I look back now, I treasure that it took forty days. It's so symbolic of who we've become and what God wanted to do. Forty days to find Him, see Him in a new light. Forty days to wander and worry were the same forty days we rallied and rested. The testimony is powerful and relatable. I can recall so many divine appointments that wouldn't have happened had that summer been one iota different.

The Measure of a Miracle

On the morning of August 1st, Pawpaw, Mawmaw and my mom went to the rehab center to bring Dad home. It wasn't a pretty sight. He had only been there six days, but his care wasn't optimal, and time was dragging on. In all, Dad lost about thirty-seven days. There were things leading up to and during his hospital stay that he would never remember. This also led to a unique perspective of time. He felt perpetually behind, always in a hurry and never able to keep up. It was going to be better for us all if he could heal at home.

The rehab facility suggested we do some in-home therapy, so they scheduled physical, occupational and speech therapy visits for the next few weeks. All the therapy personnel struggled to understand Dad's condition. Our favorite quote from this time was, "Mr. Hooper, you look horrible on paper." All the notes about my dad were very clinical and factual, but very incomplete if you hadn't met him in person. They were expecting to come and work with someone in an almost vegetative state, but Dad would meet them at the door, fill out their paperwork, do their classes and then see them out. His attention span had been affected the most. He couldn't stay with one thought or task very long without getting a major headache. While he remembered how to read, he was unable to focus for more than a paragraph at a time. He knew hot from cold and quiet from loud. Their endless questions were exhausting, but he remained a good sport and genuinely tried to cooperate.

When the last therapist visited, and we followed up with the last specialist, everyone was still ignoring the one word I wanted to use to describe the event – "miracle." Was it really that hard to admit that God had been our only hope? The final medical diagnosis mentioned that while his brain should've been affected in many ways, it turns out only one part of his brain had experienced trauma. The part that tells your body that it's ok had been damaged; so Dad wasn't ok, he just thought he was. Being unaffected or not having any lasting repercussions was not an option. They chose to interpret their facts and we chose to never accept that answer. We know Jesus a little too well. We have always known that He alone was Dad's healer, and He was the source for all the strength and peace that summer required.

What Am I Supposed to Do About That?

My life changed drastically because of dad's illness. While some factors impacted my personality and my faith, others were nothing more than decisions at the time. I didn't know I was making enormous, life-altering choices at the time, but everything decided in those days seemed to be heavy. It's funny that split second impressions can affect your entire life. The faintest of feelings can define both history and destiny.

While my dad was in his coma, he had more than one interesting encounter with what he believes was the voice of God. If you ever hear His voice, we say that you'll never be the same. When you are conscious and communing with God, you have a filter to help sort through everything you hear. But hearing God's voice in an uninhibited state is a different subject altogether. Nothing in real life prepared Dad to experience this voice. Walking away unchanged was not an option. While he heard Him say more than one thing during the forty days, this is the most important thing he remembers: I am not pleased with much of my creation.

Dad's first thought was, "What am I supposed to do about that?" It was righteous frustration, incredulous confusion. There weren't any further instructions, no details or explanation. If God is displeased, then what can we do? There's also a real element of sarcasm here. We can accept that God wants and needs more from us, but not when we can't even take ourselves to the bathroom! Why did God say this now? Why did He say it to us?

Do you know how you would respond if you believed God was displeased? The one cause and the one Person you would've given your entire life for and He was basically stopping time to tell you of his disappointment? How would you start to fix anything that was so strained? At one point in our lives, we might've had the congregation and the gumption to tackle such a difficult topic. When you speak into dozens of lives each week, you might believe that you could affect change. If you were rich, powerful, good-looking and of notoriety, then pleasing God might seem more possible. But what about when God tells you this in a broken state? As unable as you've ever been? What can one man do? When you don't know what the next day will hold, where do you even start?

From the Unknown to the Unlikely

With one statement we could've become paralyzed. The only thing that kept us going was truth. There are a few things we knew to be right. Had we not known God, His voice and His character, we would've never survived this wilderness experience. Once again, the thing that saw us through was the exact thing that would lead us on.

We believe that you must set your hand to the plow and never look back (Luke 9:62). We also know that the gifts and calling of God are without repentance, totally irrevocable (Romans 11:29). He hasn't changed His mind or forgotten about our part. This calling, ministry and assignment is as worthy as it ever has been. Dad determined that his ministry was still one of the only things worth living and dying for. Not everyone has something that they believe in so strongly, but we do. We know that service to the Lord is more important than life itself.

> No matter how lost or broken you've ever been, God still has something incredible He wants to accomplish with and through you.

From an unlikely place, at an unlikely time, you can make decisions that will positively impact the kingdom of God forever. No matter how lost or broken you've ever been, God still has something incredible He wants to accomplish with and through you. I can also admit that we've screwed up and gotten discouraged along the way too. We are far from perfect, but I believe we still strive for all the things that matter. If you find yourself in a difficult or compromising situation, when it's easier to cave than to stand, remember this: to be close to Christ, to have Him know you and to know Him intimately, is the goal of our existence. It's this type of relationship that allowed my dad to hear God so powerfully from a hospital bed. It's that confidence that kept us dedicated to a mission some would call impossible. And ultimately, it's our friendship with God that will also bring us to a point of both redemption and victory.

The LORD will perfect that which concerneth me: thy mercy, O LORD, endureth for ever: forsake not the works of thine own hands.

Psalm 138:8 (KJV)

Scary Questions and a Slippery Slope

About five weeks after Dad was released from the hospital, we were eating at one of our favorite restaurants. Just as we were getting ready to leave, my mom saw a family come in the door to be seated. We didn't know their names, but we knew their story. We had shared most of our hospital stay with them. They also had a loved one in ICU that summer, so we had spent a lot of time waiting together. Like us, their loved one had been released from the hospital a few weeks before and they were on one of their first family outings too.

The wife helped her husband to the table using the physical therapy safety belt he wore. He also required her assistance to sit down, read the menu, use a fork and eat his food. His road to recovery would be very long, so they began taking one step at a time. I wish I knew where their story went from here, but we sadly lost touch with them after that evening. I can't help but think that my dad's journey could've been similar. When we got up to walk to the car, Dad was unassisted; he walked out the door as easily as ever, but that night the other potential outcomes were more than obvious. I've never wanted to dwell on what might've made us different, but the story is incomplete without this thought.

How do you behave when you survive something others do not? How do you react to your miracle? How do I live once I've walked into my land of promise?

At the hospital, we met families coming and going. Some got to leave and go to rooms or rehabs, while others faced unexpected and sudden losses. Nothing prepares you to console others when you're in the same horrible set of circumstances. Being unable to fix others or myself made me feel so much more lost and broken; I knew I had little to no control over my outcome, but I desperately wanted to be helpful and busy. Even when I had enough faith to hang on for my miracle, I didn't have much hope left over to believe with someone else. Every negative report or uncertain result tested our patience and resolve. On the last day, when the answers finally came, I would be lying if I said I wasn't surprised. Even in my faith, I was shocked. And I was scared. My whole world began to revolve around, "What now?"

We don't understand how or why this happened. There but for the grace of God go I.

I was not entitled to a good outcome. It's dangerous to believe that we deserved a good answer. I don't think you can earn a miracle, but I know they exist, and I am in awe and humbled when I get to see one take place. They say dad recovered from his injuries because he was healthy when he got sick. His heart, kidneys, lungs and brain were able to heal themselves in many ways. Their plan of a medicated coma was to keep him still long enough to keep him safe. But what if one little piece were different? I still don't care to dive too far into the question, "Why me?" but I must respect the inquiry, so I will say this: We don't know.

"I don't know" is one of the truest answers I can share, and I am not ashamed to do so. It doesn't display a lack of faith, it just let's us all humbly and honestly move on. The fact that I will never know the answer to people's questions about this topic has finally led me to a peaceful place. I am certain that my mother and grandmother fought death and some demons from hell in the waiting room that first day. I believe my father's life was spared because dozens of our friends and family from all over the world interceded on his behalf. I know that God has numbered the days of each person on earth, so a simple thought would be that it just wasn't Dad's time. But each answer I find leads to more theologically depressing questions. I've often wondered if the other families didn't pray enough? Is this about being too holy or not holy enough? Or did God just give that person less time? If that wasn't our time, then how much time do I have left? And what am I supposed to do with it?

Many people I'm close to have lost loved ones even though they deeply believed in healing, those that held on but never received an earthly answer. Scripture teaches that God is sovereign and I know that will be the conclusion I ultimately find for everything. That answer doesn't do much to help when I'm struggling with the question though. The fact that some crazy cosmic being gets to determine who we lose and who we keep is not a safe line of questioning; I don't recommend following such discussions to their inevitable conclusions. When I started to dwell on this topic, I went to my mom. I told her about this question and the ideas I wanted to share. She has seen more than her fair share of sadness and we lived through this wilderness together. I respect her perspective, but she told me that this was nothing more than a lesson she had already learned. God can be trusted. While I want proof and to be protected from heartache, her experience shows that I'm not going to find any better answer.

I pray that these ponderings allow others to see the power of "I don't know." Seeking these answers becomes a slippery slope, one where I strive for some assurance and no longer focus on the presence of Christ. A much more helpful thought process can start once I let that go. We live every day, inviting Jesus into our circumstances. Dad was happy he had spent a lifetime living well. A history of clean living didn't hurt. Investing in the kingdom, living to lead others, serving the Lord wholeheartedly – all these things led us to walk in the favor of the Lord. I can't even imagine what this story would look like had circumstances been different, but I honestly believe that Jesus would've been in that outcome too.

If Dad's life had ended in 2005, would he have been happy with the legacy he left? With no amendments, additions or explanations, would he be content with what remained? That's easy. No. Absolutely not. Our story makes no sense without the continued work of today. The purpose of our hospital experience can only be seen from here, the other side.

Calling It Canaan

Like the children of Israel waiting in the wilderness, only a few had enough faith to see the journey through to its bitter end. After spies declared that the land was filled with giants, the whole crew had to wander in the desert for forty years because of their fear. God preserved Joshua and Caleb, their families, and lots of the young people for the Promised Land but those men of faith had to wait and wonder too.

My forty days do not perfectly compare to the exodus of Scripture, but I think this analogy applies to my life all the time. I was preserved for a purpose, but I've seen several seasons of waiting and wandering. My home and family have never been the same and the journey took us to a new and exciting place, one that we're still exploring today. The Promised Land had always been set apart for the Israelites, even foretold to their ancestor Abraham. It took them a long time to get there. The work we are doing for the Lord now was always a part of His calling on our lives, even though we didn't always see the specifics this way. It also has taken a long time for us to get here.

I have walked the width of my wilderness. I've wandered many miles. I have every right to be weary. So why am I not? How do I view this so positively all these years later? It's not because I'm over it. I wake up with nightmares. I still hear hospital beeps when it's silent and I'm alone. I sometimes stop and stare because I can smell the disinfectants and antiseptics. Every time it's hot, I'm afraid Dad is overdoing it and I follow him around with a fan and a bottle of water. Every time our life gets stressful, I think my phone is going to ring with yet another medical emergency. I live my life waiting for the next horrific reveal, the next proverbial shoe to drop. What will the world make me to face today? I am forever changed by these circumstances, but I refuse to be stuck. I find it much too easy to be jaded, so instead I struggle to believe that I have not yet told the complete story.

So how do we do this? Why in the world do we hold on? What's so special about where our forty-day experience took us? Because we know that this is Canaan. This is my Promised Land! Every single day asks me to trust Jesus a little bit more. Every breath I take is an opportunity to praise the Lord, to recognize that I couldn't even dream of being here without Him. The land and my days are not all sunshine and roses. There are still battles to fight; we are still surrounded by division and doubt. The giants we saw from the other side of the Jordan still exist, but we have chosen to tackle the future in faith and not in fear. In the actual Promised Land of Scripture, the people dwelt with God. They inhabited a place that belonged to them, they walked in God's provision and relied upon Him daily. Being at the right place offset the trials they faced. That invitation remains today. God's not inviting me to something totally unknown. He's been here before, with hundreds of thousands of other believers. He's doing something new in my life, leading me to something beyond my wildest imagination, but walking by faith is not new to the Gospel way.

We are walking into a place we've never been. Why God led us here, how we got here when others didn't, or what the big plan might be; I'm not sure. I don't think those are the questions I've needed to ask. I've avoided this topic for more than a decade now because I didn't want to find the answers. I feel the Lord saying that I should make myself at home on this wild, new ride. I should settle into the questions instead of running from them and let Him reveal the answers only in the proper times. He's not concerned about the resolution; He's into the reveal. My faith has a destination, but I think the Gospel was for the journey. In this place where I still feel a little scared, I've finally started to feel a little free. I can see the promises unfolding before my eyes. I see pieces coming together; Scripture is being fulfilled, truth is being proclaimed and lives are being changed. I feel welcome here. This is home. Welcome to a place that I call Canaan, population: me.

The Mission to Ministry

We remain faithful to the vision the Lord has entrusted into our hands. That's not just a ten-year vision… it's all my future plans. It's whatever God has spent multiple generations preparing us for. I'm ready for specific instruction, but I am also content with the next simple step. God has given us plenty to do while we wait for Him to lead the way, while we wrestle with daily life and while we walk our path of faith.

He has called us to be ministers, meant to bring true ministry to the people we serve. We make sure people encounter Jesus in real ways, when and where they need Him most. God has also said that we will bring people to a point of decision, whether for salvation or submission. If you're looking to follow Christ, we'd love to journey with you. Step one or step ten thousand, it's a privilege to be in pursuit with the people of God. He promised that we would play a vital role in a revival that stripped away the religious masquerade we've become accustomed to; we would help set this land on fire for Him. He told us that our area is like a burned-over field and we will get to experience its fruitful harvest in due season. We know that He will use us to repair broken roads and restore strained relationships. He has created us for this; the big, little and in between have prepared us for right now.

He has created us for this; the big, little and in between have prepared us for right now.

It's impossible to say that we've never doubted God's call or all these words, but after our hospital experience and a summer in the wilderness, we know how to hang on. We feel as able today as ever before (Joshua 14:11-13). We must be honest about the fear and uncertainty we faced when it was time to dig back in. But God has not changed His mind about us, and after everything I've seen, I won't be prone to change my mind about Him.

PART II
Chapter Six

Lesson One
Love the Lord in Spirit and Truth

"Master, which is the great commandment in the law?"
Jesus said unto him, "Thou shalt love the Lord thy God with all thy heart, and with all thy soul, and with all thy mind. This is the first and great commandment. And the second is like unto it, 'Thou shalt love thy neighbor as thyself.' On these two commandments hang all the law and the prophets."

Matthew 22:36-40 (KJV)

Return to the Altar

How do you keep track of everything the Lord has done? Sometimes mine is a running list on the last page of a devotional; other times it's a white board brain dump before a season of fasting and prayer at my church. I would have to say that most commonly though, the things that the Lord has done for me are simply engraved on my heart, imprinted in my mind. They are with me always, but never easy for everyone to see.

I think the Lord is constantly at work, but we only see bits and pieces of His efforts on our behalf. If we knew everything that went on in the spiritual realm, we'd be more scared than grateful. It is in graceful protection that we are sheltered from the worst life has to offer.

And he went on his journeys from the south even to Bethel, unto the place where his tent had been at the beginning, between Bethel and Hai; Unto the place of the altar, which he had made there at the first: and there Abram called on the name of the LORD.

Genesis 13:3-4 (KJV)

When I read the above portion of Scripture the other day, I started thinking about how God works with man. In this Genesis account, Abram and Sarai had traveled to Egypt to avoid a famine in their land. To save his own life, Abram said that Sarai was his sister and Sarai went to join the pharaoh's harem. When the Lord came down and plagued the entire royal family because of the lie, Abram, with Sarai and their entire family, were exiled and forced to leave Egypt. When they had nowhere to go, they went back and found the place they had last heard God speak. Abram went to find his altar.

Abram's altar. A place of great sacrifice, something costly, dirty, nasty and hard. A place where He met His Master, and the place that forever changed his destiny. Sometimes it's hard to go back to life-altering scenes, but it's necessary to dwell there until we see the purpose and are invited beyond and into something new. Andy Stanley says, "Experience doesn't make you wiser. Evaluated experience makes you wiser." It is responsible to remember; it's imperative to analyze and adapt.

Abram could only move forward after he revisited his past. He checked his beliefs, reviewed his shortcomings, walked out a new kind of repentance and reminded himself of the promises of God. But most importantly, back at his altar, meeting God again inspired him to continue his journey of faith.

In the days after Dad's hospital experience, we spent a lot of time reestablishing our altars. We had to revisit every decision we had ever made. Would we continue the ministry? How would life look different than before? What could we drop, or what should we keep? When would life feel normal again?

My dad will be the first to tell you that this line of thinking was the most overwhelming part of his recovery. If you faced the fear of dying at any moment, how would you live differently? His biggest question dealt with priorities. If something is important enough to do, then it's important enough to do no matter what. However, if something is not of life-or-death importance, then we must ask ourselves why it's worth our time at all. To make every day matter, you must spend your most valuable commodity of time in only the most important of ways.

Since Dad's recovery was far from textbook perfect, we were unsure of how reality would affect him. What happened when he got stressed that first time? Is it possible to avoid all high-pressure situations? It's unlikely that life would be easy, but now we had been shaken and we were unsure of ourselves. When we say we never doubted God, that is very true. But to say we faithfully trusted enough to not worry or doubt ourselves and others, that would be untrue. We never shied away from difficult situations, but now we weren't sure we could handle just anything life would throw our way.

We were only able to hear and obey God's commands because we went back and waited where we belonged.

Instead of facing all the possibilities on our own, we went back to the last place we found Jesus. It wasn't necessarily a location, but more of a mindset. We went back to the last thing the Lord told us to do, and we proposed to seek His face and wait until He spoke otherwise. Over the last thirteen years, God has given us further direction and some things have changed, but we were only able to hear and obey those commands because we went back and waited where we belonged.

The last thing we knew the Lord had promised was in our church and in our family. We were meant to stick together, and we were meant to establish something in Frisco. No matter how much we wanted to leave or how little sense it all made, we had to return to the place we were called. So, we did just that. We taught and sang and prayed and led to the best of our ability while we also recovered – emotionally, physically, mentally, relationally. There was a lot to process in those first few months, but the Lord honored our efforts and never left us alone. I think because we went searching for Him, He made it easy to be found.

This I recall to my mind; Therefore, I have hope. Through the Lord's mercies we are not consumed, Because His compassions fail not. They are new every morning; Great is Your faithfulness. 'The LORD is my portion,' says my soul, 'Therefore I hope in Him!' The LORD is good to those who wait for Him, To the soul who seeks Him. It is good that one should hope and wait quietly For the salvation of the LORD.
Lamentations 3:21-26 (NKJV)

For those who have waited on and placed their hope in the Lord, there is a special blessing. Something unique to this divine relationship can be found in our searching. Those that seek, find.

Those that ask, receive. Those that knock, enter. Promise after promise keeps pouring off the pages of my Bible.

No doubt, I'm called to find the Lord. For me personally, I find Him best in the floor of my bathroom or around my family's dining room table or in my quiet office at church. I go to one of these sacred places and I remember everything that the Lord has done for me. I don't need all the answers. I don't need every future plan. I just need Him. He is enough. Only when I go back and recall everything He has said and done can I be ready to move forward. So, the first place God asked us to go after the hospital was back to where we came from, to simply do all that He had said up until that point. It was scary at times, uncomfortable too, but He didn't waste a single day. We were not regressing; this was His version of progress. Not in our efforts. Not by my expectations. Not in my timing or in my own way, but in our obedience and by His grace alone. Only God can redeem things in this way. Only I can tell my story. Only He deserves the glory that this will bring.

Making Reservations

My father was forty-seven years old when he ended up spending a summer in the hospital because of a heat stroke and brain bleed. Just before this tragedy happened, he had been helping a new ministry get started. Several young men had been hurt by a local church after an internship never turned into promised staff positions. These boys had given a few years of their life to the ministry and were feeling discouraged and passed over.

Our meeting them happened at a very good time; my dad had been looking for the catalyst that would kick-start the next phase of our ministry and they were in desperate need of a mentor and friend. I hadn't signed on to help my family in the church yet. At that time, I would've never admitted that I felt called or drawn to the ministry at all. Taking on the church, both for services and in daily operations during my dad's illness, was what started all of that. My realization of my calling was one of many results of our wilderness experience. More about that later.

"True success requires a successor." If you believe that, then finding young people to pour into and asking Jesus to send you leaders in need makes sense. Dad has always enjoyed providing people with a platform. Even before his hospital stay, he wanted to leave a legacy. I think my family always knew that our family legacy was safe with me, but when it came to looking for capable hands that could handle the ministry, I had yet to prove myself.

I have mentioned before that Dad heard the voice of Jesus a few times throughout the twenty-eight days he was technically/medically unconscious. The first thing he heard was his name and the disappointing statement, "I'm not pleased with much of my creation." No matter how useless that made him feel, he distinctly remembers that voice and those words. He is also just as sure about the next thing Jesus said:

"Everything has not already been said or done. I have reserved a few things just for this generation."

In that moment, he saw a flip chart of photos. Faces of the young men he had been mentoring flickered by, followed by images of me and my cousins. Most all the younger people my dad had a relationship with were given some screen time in this mental presentation for his eyes only. This new challenge was meant to stir excitement in the aftermath of great disappointment. Even though the Lord's first sentence was full of hurt, this second thought proves that He was far from through with us and that we were still supposed to affect our community.

For if you keep silent at this time, relief and deliverance will rise for the Jews from another place, but you and your father's house will perish. And who knows whether you have not come to the kingdom for such a time as this?

Esther 4:14 (ESV)

I can't help but be reminded of this verse in Esther when our heroine is finally assured of her purpose. In one of the lowest parts of her story, Esther is reminded that she was born for a reason, something special and divine; her people would survive captivity because of her bravery. She was not a mistake and not one detail of her story had gone unnoticed. Her city was right, her dwelling was right, her influence was right. Accurate, correct, perfect and proper. God's involvement in Esther's life was unmistakable, but only in hindsight. In case you were wondering, that is the way life always works.

The trials we face today are nothing like what our forefathers dealt with and they do not resemble what our great-grandchildren will have to handle. I expect things to grow crazier than we could ever prepare them for. We can't anticipate how different even the next few months will be for our world, so it is vital that we build on the firm foundation of the Lord and His principles. We should instill truth in our own life and it's imperative that we reach the young ones coming up behind us (whether they be our own children or other young believers the Lord has sent our way).

Here are a few of those principles I think we all need to accept. They are timeless; convictions strong enough to hold us together when everything falls apart. Some work quickly, while others may take generations to establish. This list is also far from exhaustive because each page of the Bible holds dozens of promises if we would only open our eyes to see them. If we are willing and able to apply God's truth, then I pray that we are also courageous enough to teach them.

- Seed, time and harvest. (Genesis 8:22)
  As long as time exists, God's kingdom and this earth will both be governed by this fact.
- The first shall be last. (Matthew 20:16)
  In the upside-down economy of God, position has very little to do with power.
- A leader must love and serve. (Mark 10:35-41)
  Nothing is too much or too little when the Lord is the one asking.
- Die to find life. (Matthew 16:24-25)
  He who freely gives his life can gain the world without losing his soul.

- The greatest revenge is love. (Matthew 5:43-44)
  The beauty of this is how a lack of vengeance is unexpected.
- Give and it will be given unto you. (Luke 6:38)
  You may have to sacrifice, but you cannot out-give God.
- Foolish things will shame the wise. (1 Corinthians 1:27)
  Jesus delights in the simple things; that's why trust is priceless but free.
- Couple honor with thanksgiving. (Psalm 50:23)
  That which you honor will overtake you, but that which you dishonor will never be found.

Those are only a few examples of the truth we've chosen to build upon. Our past, present and future are undeniably marked by these ideas. I believe there are great things awaiting the millennial church, but we must stay put and plug in. The young church leaders do not have time to learn everything the hard way, and I don't believe the kingdom of God has ever been established by novices and prideful prodigies. First-hand experience is valuable, but being willing to hear wisdom is an even better trait to desire.

The future will be different, but I believe an undeniable move of God is on its way. I believe it will involve revival and repentance, a church that fights for rigorous honesty and grace-filled community. Politics, business, industry, war, slavery, sexuality, poverty and disease will all be discussed openly instead of minimized or swept under a rug. God's next outpouring will also be something sacred and holy, a place or movement where sin isn't tolerated, and we admit just how far Jesus had to come to save fallen man. We will be disgusted by our sin but overwhelmed by our God. I believe the Lord is seeking people He can use, vessels that are willing to carry His power and anointing. Those are heavy words, but this is an important issue.

Jesus promised something new. He said that whatever awaits us will be unique, something not already seen and not already done. He's waiting for a group to rise and bridge the gap, a band of believers more concerned with interceding than entertaining. It won't be because of who we are, what we know or where we're from. In fact, the grace of the matter is that He isn't even basing this future blessing on our abilities or our opinions or whether we have earned or deserved His attention. He is getting ready to move again, in and through us, simply because it's time. My qualifications are trust and surrender; Jesus will provide me with everything else. If something has been saved for this generation, I'm willing to step out in faith, with courage, and boldly claim my reservation.

Chapter Seven

Lesson Two
Never Doubt, Always Hope

"And not only this, but [with joy] let us exult in our sufferings and rejoice in our hardships, knowing that hardship (distress, pressure, trouble) produces patient endurance; and endurance, proven character (spiritual maturity); and proven character, hope and confident assurance [of eternal salvation]. Such hope [in God's promises] never disappoints us, because God's love has been abundantly poured out within our hearts through the Holy Spirit who was given to us."

Romans 5:3-5 (AMP)

Meant for My Harm, Used for My Good

There is no way I could've ever foreseen how different my life would be after one summer. When I was a child, my summer days were filled with quintessential Small Town, USA moments – fireflies, fireworks, free time and family. Those times laid a pretty great foundation for me and I'm grateful for the groundwork my childhood built, but I'm also a bit overwhelmed at how necessary that stable base has been.

Dad's wilderness experience and hospital stay caused me to redefine what I wanted most in this life. Keeping our church doors open and finishing school became more important than finding a career and choosing a life path or crafting a five-year plan. A great temptation at that point in my life was also to fight for my independence. Instead of focusing on myself, I was forced to admit my deficiencies and start to live honestly with others. It taught me that the best parts of life happen in the valleys. We are graced with good times too; I'm privileged enough to recognize my blessings and rejoice over each one. But real life is filled with lower lows than you think you can handle. My reality forced me to dig deeper, and only then was I able to survive.

A Scripture from Joseph's life comes to mind. I've never been thrown into a pit, disowned by my family, sold into slavery, or stuck in a prison so Joseph's use of the word "harm" might skew things a little. However, I am sure that this is a godly truth, so I don't mind viewing my circumstances through this lens.

You intended to harm me, but God intended it all for good. He brought me to this position, so I could save the lives of many people.

Genesis 50:20 (NLT)

Without my so-called "wilderness experience," I probably would've lived up to everyone's expectations. Now I choose to defy them, but I mean that with all the kindness I can muster. Without the summer of 2005, I would probably be employed in an artistic field, living a life way above my current means. I would probably have great health insurance, a nice car, a retirement account, and I might've landed no telling where with new friends, new hobbies and new favorite foods. I agree that this is all speculation, but I ask that you oblige me for a few more paragraphs.

I could've built any life I wanted. I believe I am capable of anything. I'm an innovative problem solver that has developed enough tact and has found enough grace to communicate and lead others well. I figure my relentless, change-the-world mentality and my unwavering confidence would've followed me no matter where I went. Stretching a little farther with the "what ifs" or "what might have been," I could've had a husband or two and a few kids by now. I could've survived as an average church attender. I don't think my faith would've faltered, but my faithfulness might've failed. Without my calling, I wouldn't sort dirty clothes, evangelize hot streets, enjoy visiting the sick and feeble and dying. My life could've been filled with expensive, extravagant and enviable things. But all those attractive accouterments fall a little flat when I look at my options today.

Now, I get to use all my gifts and talents to serve others. It's a pleasure to choose this path. I can see that my art degree, my hobbies, my odd jobs and my interests aren't wasted. Living sacrificially and putting all my preconceived notions aside, I am now at a place where I can lead groups closer to Christ, teaching them what it means to love like Jesus. It's an honor to follow Him so others can follow me. Stumbling and struggling is a part of that reality that I hope to bear with more grace each day, but I'm honored to do this to let people see how genuinely authentic faith can be. I am seeing my neighbors and my world change all the time! I can't guarantee that all the things that bring me fulfillment now would've been a part of that other life. Where I am today may not meet everyone's expectations, but I can guarantee that this reality is no less extraordinary. I believe that this is where I was meant to be all along.

When sickness tried to take my family…
When the hospital visit could've derailed generations worth of ministerial efforts…
When one summer threatened every plan, I had ever made…

Out of the pain and the ashes, something beautiful was born. God's work in my life since those days is nothing short of miraculous. I see divinity on every single page of my story. I would not be who I am, be where I'm at, or be doing what I am doing without all those supposedly harmful situations. The hurts and disappointments I've experienced made me who I am and I'm happier than I thought I could be. Rehashing this journey for everyone to read has been a vital part of my healing. Only in hindsight am I able to prove that God is good. I knew and felt it at the time (that's one of the reasons you persevere and survive), but I can tell others about it now. God's writing a testimony on the pages of my heart that is spilling onto the pages of this book and it's a story I can't explain without Him. God's ultimate goal is glory. His glory is what saves a soul. His glory is what establishes a kingdom. If I hope to be a part of His plan, I must first learn to find His glory. His glory is good.

For me, I have been brought to this place and to this time to play a vital role in the salvation of many people. Saved from sin, saved from sorrow or simply saved from themselves, I love the fact that I get to be an ambassador of God's grace in troubled times. And I don't just have empty platitudes to give when I reach out to them. From a place of my scars, I can relate with care and compassion. I can also guide with help and hope. Trying to make people achieve

> *If we desire to see people changed by God's grace and for His glory, then we must acknowledge the messiness of reality and choose to stick around until we see the something good.*

perfection is impossible; saying that everything is neat or pretty helps no one. If we desire to see people changed by God's grace and for His glory, then we must acknowledge the icky messiness of reality and choose to stick around until we see the something good. Upon surrender to God, He was able to take all my experiences and masterfully create something good from them.

Craftsmanship takes time; seeds need the darkness of the soil to get ready for harvest. Not growing weary in well-doing is the greatest challenge of life today; believing that God will use this is easier on paper than it is in the broken world I'm trying to reach by building relationships. I am God's work-in-progress. May this journey exceed people's expectations and defy the odds. He's building something worth showing off, so I will no longer regret my harm. My testimony is unique, but I will no longer apologize for it. I will rejoice in the good, I will praise until the mountains move and I will be here when there is more of a story to tell.

Keeping On

Many of my years have been centered around the church and working in the ministry. My parents were pastors before I was born, so I've always participated in a system of beliefs that they approved of. As I got older, I was presented with the same challenge that confronts almost every other teen or young adult. Will I live for Jesus because they do? Or do I want to see what life is like for myself?

In a time when we have millennials leaving the church in droves and every new preacher on the block trying to redefine religion, I think it's important for me to distinguish my journey of faith. I have seen too much to ever doubt God's existence. My crisis came when I had to reimagine the purpose of my faith. How did Jesus want my life to look? Had I ever given Him the right to direct my life? I could believe in God with almost no questions asked, but it was going to take many more decisions and much more effort if I was to be used by Him.

After graduating from high school, I enrolled in art college. Explaining the paradigm shift for a preacher's kid from a private Christian school to a liberal arts school could be summarized by saying, "It was rough."

After trying my hand at graphic design and multimedia development, I finally settled in on video and audio production. The degree I completed was a great choice for me, but making friends and fitting in didn't come easily. The atmosphere wasn't very conducive to my faith, but somehow, I became more determined about my personal beliefs every day. Turns out, it was the perfect setting to work out a lot of my beliefs before they would be tested in real life.

In June 2005, when everything changed for us, I one semester of school left. I was in a senior-level class, compiling my portfolio and preparing for job interviews and graduation. I knew that even though my family was in crisis, my education must be completed.

If my dad woke up from a coma to find I had quit school, we'd have been preparing for my funeral and not his.

In retrospect, I see that maintaining daily operations was an act of faith. Whether I was completing projects, going to school or paying the bills, I tried to act normally. These simple things were daily proof that somewhere deep down I knew life was going to go on. My efforts were the substance of what I was hoping for, the evidence of things I could not yet see. This trying time was a momentary pause, but it was nowhere near the end. I'd like to think I consciously chose this profound truth, but it wasn't anything that revolutionary. It was more of an internal prompting that I was unwilling to give up on.

Continuing my dad's work became my mission and it's a decision that marks my life even today. I went to church that first Sunday morning, only three days after admitting Dad to the hospital. Sure, our entire congregation knew what was going on, but the church doors should be open, right? They'd never been closed. My family skipped vacations for years and even drove home sometimes in the middle of a Saturday night to be sure we were there every single Sunday morning.

Until then, I had never taught a sermon and I had only sung with my family. When I got up to lead the service that morning, it's a miracle I could say anything at all. The message was short, something about David and the giant or Joshua and a big wall… yep, we were reliving my favorite Veggie Tales analogies with as much reverence as I could muster. There was no formal application and I never had papers to file, but I'm pretty sure I became interim senior pastor that day.

Choosing to do church that morning had life-long repercussions. It meant that I would go back every week and do what I felt was right. I can't recollect the exact moment I decided to keep going. There wasn't a bright shining light or a burning plant. I decided to do something harder than continue; I decided not to quit. Does anyone else see the difference in that? Deciding to continue versus deciding not to quit; it's the same conclusion with different, life-altering motives.

When I decided not to quit, that meant that I would face whatever hardship would come my way. Deciding to stay seems passive to me. Continuing wasn't the key. It's more powerful to choose not to leave. A reason to quit stared me in the face each morning. The option to find another life, run away and find anything else to do is quite an attractive offer when your world is crumbling.

But I didn't quit, and I didn't leave. With other places to go and other things to do, I stayed. The power to choose was mine. I had made the wise, yet difficult decision. This new, scary place was part of God's purpose and this crazy circumstance somehow felt natural

With other places to go and other things to do, I stayed.

during the chaos. I'm so happy that I knew where to turn for this perspective. All those Bible verses and Sunday school songs replay in your heart when you need them most. Consider this promise.

You will show me the way of life, granting me the joy of your presence and the pleasures of living with you forever.

Psalm 16:11 (NLT)

God's way was going to be best. I was walking in His will without even realizing it. I was doing what felt right and natural, but those were instincts developed by a faith I had been cultivating for more than twenty years. I know that all of His promises are true, but I still struggle with the waiting trust requires. In the wilderness, His perfect plan for me was to stay put, to stand firm on the foundation He was building and to listen for further instructions.

During my heartbreak, I was experiencing the beauty of His joy. His presence has forever affected me. As we healed, I saw His handiwork at every turn. If we've seen difficulties, they have made us stronger. Standing still and waiting is always harder than moving forward or going your own way, but it's worth it. Taking a stand, not leaving when I had every right to, made me tackle every worry and conquer all my fears. I had plenty of reason to doubt, but the Lord had birthed in me a resilient hope. One found through endurance, one that's uncommon but true. My hope is a confident assurance in who God is and how good He can be. Now, with more than a decade behind me, I must believe that I made an excellent decision, one that I couldn't regret even if I wanted to.

Chapter Eight

Lesson Three
Follow the Instructions of the Word

"How can a young man cleanse his way? By taking heed according to Your word. With my whole heart I have sought You; Oh, let me not wander from Your commandments! Your word I have hidden in my heart, That I might not sin against You."

Psalm 119:9-11 (NKJV)

Committed into His Hands

Each person in my family had a different reaction to daily life that summer. Mom and Mawmaw camped outside in the waiting room for about twenty-two hours a day. They would take a break to race home and shower or change, but never at the same time. Almost every waking and sleeping moment found them there. I balanced everything quite well (in my humble opinion), going from school to church to family to hospital for the forty days. My aunts and uncles held down their jobs and homes but came and spent as much time with us as possible. Cousins, relatives, friends, parishioners, all took time out of their daily lives to help us whenever they could.

And then there was Pawpaw.

Pawpaw stayed with us in the waiting room that first day, but quickly went back to work. There were yards to mow, trees to trim, rental property to maintain, churches to manage, people to meet and many other daily tasks that still had to be done. He was waiting on the Lord, but His waiting looked a whole lot different than mine.

Although he wasn't preachy about it back then, we've come to learn why he responded that way.

Therefore do not be ashamed of the testimony of our Lord or of me His prisoner, but join with me in suffering for the gospel according to the power of God, who has saved us and called us with a holy calling, not according to our works, but according to His own purpose and grace which was granted us in Christ Jesus from all eternity, but now has been revealed by the appearing of our Savior Christ Jesus, who abolished death and brought life and immortality to light through the gospel, for which I was appointed a preacher and an apostle and a teacher. For this reason, I also suffer these things, but I am not ashamed; for I know whom I have believed, and I am convinced that He is able to guard what I have entrusted to Him until that day.

2 Timothy 1:8-12 (NASB, emphasis mine)

The point Paul was making, and the principle Pawpaw lived by, was this: God can guard anything we entrust into His hands. When my daddy was 7 days old, in 1958, Pawpaw took him to church and dedicated him to the Lord. While those ceremonies can be a lot of tradition, pomp and circumstance, this action was the first thing my granddad recalled about my father. In reality, Dad wasn't ours. We didn't have to understand what was going on; we didn't have to intervene. Dad had been committed to the Lord long ago, and then when He decided to serve God and become a minister of the Gospel in 1979, he had just reaffirmed that calling.

The J.B. Phillips' translation of 2 Timothy 1:12 says, "For I know the one in whom I have placed my confidence, and I am perfectly certain that the work he has committed to me is safe in his hands until that day." Where would we have been if we didn't know the Lord?

Pawpaw stood at the foot of a bed in the ICU and confirmed what he had said more than forty-five years prior. He told the Lord, "I dedicated him to You at seven days old. If You need him worse than I do, then you can have him." Those forty years of faith had prepared him for this moment. He knew that God didn't take people and that God was not to blame for this problem. He knew that everything we were going through was an attack of the enemy; Satan had come to steal, kill and destroy us (John 10:10). But when you're fighting for your life (or the life of a loved one), you must believe first-hand that Jesus can handle anything you're facing. Whether Dad lived or died, we had given God control of our lives and He was going to see us through. Y'all, it was too late to turn back now.

"*I dedicated him to You at 7 days old. If You need him worse than I do, then You can have him.*"

Once Pawpaw settled this in his heart, he returned to work. Sadly, he was supposed to make sure the grass they were laying survived the sweltering summer heat, but alas even against his best efforts, that stupid grass died. We don't even have a green backyard as a trophy for our trying times. There were many other things to keep him busy, so that's what he did. He visited. He transported. He prayed. He was still vigilant and ever a part of the family, but his waiting would not be done in a room. His faith was not built of his efforts, but he didn't want to be stuck with idle hands either.

I spoke to him about his feelings when I started writing the memoir, asking him to remember the emotion of those days. For the first time, I understood that this didn't come naturally. He worked and kept busy because he had to, and he felt there was no choice. It only looked like an act of super faith, but the choice was moment-by-moment. It was painful for him and the daily pressure was intense. He said, "It's like you were walking around in a daze. You were at home trying to work, but also trying to figure out if any of it even mattered anymore. Without Johnny, what would we really do?"

We don't dwell on that possibility too often. We knew the gravity of the situation, but time has numbed some of those pains.

On day twenty-eight, when Dad woke up from his coma, Pawpaw tells it best. "We knew they were going to try and start waking him up sometime. But everything had dragged on and there were sometimes they tried and had no luck. Then one day, the phone rings and a real, serious guy says, 'Mr. Hooper, I've got someone who wants to speak to you.' And a scratchy, quiet voice comes on the line and says, 'Hi, Dad.' You knew it was coming, or at least you thought it was. You prayed that this was real, but time practically stands still until you get down there and see it for yourself."

Just see for yourself. The day you always believed would come, but that no one could guarantee. Get in the car. Drive as fast as you can. Find your family and the doctors. Then go into a room that others had not come out of and see for yourself.

I believe that's been the invitation from the beginning. Life with God is about the experience. My task has always been to find the joy in the journey. My destination is secure, but there's much to be done along the way. When Jesus first met his apostles and they began following Him, they asked, "Rabbi, where are you staying?" Jesus' answer is recorded in John 1:39 (NLT). "'Come and see,' he said. It was about four o'clock in the afternoon when they went with him to the place where he was staying, and they remained with him the rest of the day."

An invite like that was too good to pass up, but whatever they found caused them to stick around. My relationship with God sounds a lot like that. In all His goodness, He has invited me to abundant and eternal life. We must give up all our baggage to find true peace in Him, but what we gain is worth anything we may lose. He is still waiting to be involved in my daily life, waiting for my invitation in response to His. Come and see. Follow Me.

Recovery Requires Community

Lone sheep are easy prey.

That's what my dad would tell you. He learned it on the farm and in years of counseling young ministers. If the choice is to go it alone or have people help you, it's always best to choose the way that brings encouragement, support, accountability, prayer partners and fellowship.

Now it's funny to hear myself say this. I'm not known for my social life or my extroverted tendencies. I've been much more independent in my life, convinced I didn't really need anyone's help. I have built walls and defenses, ignorantly believing that life is better if you don't have to trust people. I have evidence of being lied about and lied to. If you've ever met another human being, you might also agree that getting close to other people can hurt. But no matter how hard I try, I can't see this playing out very well. Historically and spiritually, there is strength in numbers.

Having other people know and love you for your weaknesses gives you a special kind of power. There's no sin that can hold you if you have a group to whom you can honestly confess. There's no obstacle too large if you have someone that can tackle it with you. There's no dream you can't accomplish if you're willing to let each member of the body play their assigned role.

The idea of needing others plays out all through the Scriptures. Here are a few favorites:

How good and pleasant it is when God's people live together in unity!

Psalm 133:1 (NIV)

Finally, all of you should be of one mind. Sympathize with each other. Love each other as brothers and sisters. Be tenderhearted and keep a humble attitude.

1 Peter 3:8 (NLT)

For where two or three are gathered together in my name, there am I in the midst of them.

Matthew 18:20 (KJV)

Carry one another's burdens; in this way you will fulfill the law of Christ.

Galatians 6:2 (HCSB)

All these verses emphasize the need for Christians to walk and work together. I really wonder now if anything was meant to be handled alone? When Jesus ascended, He left the Holy Spirit with the church. It was His intention that people be led by the Spirit and go through life together. If the apostles needed each other, then who am I to think I will be fine on my own?

Times of crisis, like our hospitalized wilderness experience, just prove this point. What would we have done without everyone that stood by us? We needed dozens of people praying. We needed help keeping the church doors open and food on our table. From simple visits and short conversations to people giving us rides and covering some expenses to even offering to stay hours and days on end at the hospital, every person was used by God. When I started to begrudge needing the help, I became very convicted. We remove someone else's purpose from God's plan when we try to do more than what we were created for.

Since these days, I've had many positive and negative experiences with people. It's messy when you dive deep with another person in life. To know and be known can really hurt when people lie or judge or leave. Despite the fear that rises in me when I talk about community, I know that I have no choice but to face the mess and hope for the best. There is a group of people out there waiting for me to be me. They will see all my burdens as blessings. They will want to know everything about my life, and they will rejoice with me as opposed to standing in judgment over me.

We remove someone else's purpose from God's plan when we try to do more than what we were created for.

Only when I walk in Christ-like humility can I conquer these problems. I believe that honesty draws honest people, vulnerability promotes vulnerability, and hope fuels hope. When I dare to live like a member of this divine tribe, I can find those other people that are willing to be there too. We must continue to trust every step of our journey to Jesus. He brings all the right people, to all the right places, at all the right times, to work in all the right ways. Just like when we had a role to play in someone else's life, we must be open to the workings of God when He uses others in ours.

Just off the top of my head, I remember close friends, distant relatives and so many people from our past and our present that made an appearance during Dad's hospital stay. We had people offer to sing songs and read the Bible over us. One group started an international prayer chain that reached all the way to Nigeria. Others brought dinner. A few people that visited were old church friends; they had moved on to other ministries, but their visits with us remain very vivid in our minds. People we've known for more than fifty years and those that we had just met each played an important role during our time of need.

Never underestimate the good you can do by just being you. The Lord has called us each to a place and a time for a purpose. The goal is for every follower of Christ to listen and obey. It's not always just for our good. Many times, there's a reason He needs us to be ready. He gets the glory when we speak into the life of a waitress. He can use every single word we share with our coworkers. He can even use our silent presence to minister to someone watching and listening for the slightest sign of hope. Again, it's never about our abilities and actions, it's about what a surrendered vessel can accomplish for the Most High God.

Every single piece of the puzzle must be there for the scene to make sense. Every single role must be filled for the show to go on. And every single moment of my life must be given over to God for Him to work with as He pleases. It's only then, in every little way, that He can lead us to redemption. Reconciliation and recovery is ours, but it's too important of a job to pursue alone. Who does God have for you to meet today?

A Lock and a Key

Can you admit to ever feeling stuck? Like life is happening all throughout a home, but you're the one hanging out in a hallway. I always told the Lord that I would go through any door He opened, but sometimes I don't see the possibilities. I'm even one of those people that looks for windows left ajar and holes sawed in the roof. I'll be the first to admit that God can work in unique and mysterious ways, and because He is a good God, I would follow Him anywhere.

I want to see forward motion in my life. I want my days to be marked by progress, but reality sometimes forces me to see that I am stuck. I'm physically free and able to do anything I please, but spiritually I might be waiting a bit more than I anticipated.

While Dad was in the hospital, he was given a wonderful vision about keys and locks. I say keys first, because in his vision, we had many more keys than we had locks to put them in. Basically, in that hallway of life, there were only a few shut doors, but we had a whole ring of keys. Each door we wanted to go through required us to analyze which key would fit best. To us, the keys represented godly principles, experiences, Scriptures, answers and information. The locks represented situations and circumstances that we needed to be involved in or get out of. When it came time for action, we had to use all our keys to unlock whatever problem we were facing.

Sometimes, you'll stand before a lock with no key to match. You'll be waiting in the presence of a decision with no definitive answer. At other times, you'll spend years of your life collecting keys with no lock in sight. Everything is open and there's no confusion, worry or doubt. Both of those times prepare us for the remainder of our life.

I don't really go around looking for keys and locks; it's more how I view life. Everything has a lock and key potential. Life doesn't stay one way forever. We will always find locks we didn't anticipate, and we'll be using keys we never thought we'd need. In all of God's wisdom, He prepares every step of our way. Walking in full surrender to God is the only way I can be sure that my life will work. He knows what I'm going to need and when I'm going to need it. He's never early and never late… even when it hurts, He is always right on time.

You can see examples of this everyday:

When you buy that book that sits on the shelf for two years, but then has the perfect message you need on the day you finally pick it up.

When you're counseling a friend through a hard time and you end up quoting the exact portion of the Bible you've been studying.

When a deadline for something you want passes, but you don't even miss what you thought you wanted when you finally receive what God had in mind.

When you live by your principles and convictions and the Lord uses those earlier decisions on your part to take you where He's always needed you to go.

When you take a wrong turn on a trip or stop at the unusual coffee shop for a snack and end up being used by the Lord to witness or help others.

Encountering the lock isn't a problem when the Lord has supplied the key. We can all get discouraged when we're asked to wait without understanding why. We can also be a little disgruntled when we must work for things we thought would come easily. Whether we are waiting or working, we can never lose sight of the fact that God still supplies all the answers.

I want to be like Caleb, the friend of Joshua. His journey to the Promised Land should've taken no more than two months but ended up requiring forty years because of his fellow Israelites' fear and unbelief. When it came time to possess the land, Caleb stepped up to receive his inheritance. His mindset was simple. With a life marked by faith, he fully followed God.

Then the sons of Judah drew near to Joshua in Gilgal, and Caleb the son of Jephunneh the Kenizzite said to him, 'You know the word which the Lord spoke to Moses the man of God concerning you and me in Kadesh-barnea. I was forty years old when Moses the servant of the Lord sent me from Kadesh-barnea to spy out the land, and I brought word back to him as it was in my heart. Nevertheless, my brethren who went up with me made the heart of the people melt with fear; but I followed the Lord my God fully. So, Moses swore on that day, saying, 'Surely the land on which your foot has trodden will be an inheritance to you and to your children forever, because you have followed the Lord my God fully.' Now behold, the Lord has let me live, just as He spoke, these forty-five years, from the time that the Lord spoke this word to Moses, when Israel walked in the wilderness; and now behold, I am eighty-five years old today. I am still as strong today as I was in the day Moses sent me; as my strength was then, so my strength is now, for war and for going out and coming in. Now then, give me this hill country about which the Lord spoke on that day, for you heard on that day that Anakim were there, with great fortified cities; perhaps the Lord will be with me, and I will drive them out as the Lord has spoken.' So Joshua blessed him and gave Hebron to Caleb the son of Jephunneh for an inheritance. Therefore, Hebron became the inheritance of Caleb the son of Jephunneh the Kenizzite until this day, because he followed the Lord God of Israel fully.

Joshua 14:6-14 (NASB)

After Dad got out of the hospital, we began categorizing certain things in our life as keys. We had survived this experience for some reason, and one of these days, we'll see what He'll use that key for. We had given our life to the study of the Word, and

God will again bring all things to our remembrance when it's time for us to share. Even when I didn't see any locks in my life, I kept collecting keys – learning new things, meeting new people, trying to positively change and be ready for whatever comes next. And now, while I'm praising God in my life's hallway, staring at a lock I can't pick nor pry, I fiddle with my keys and ask Him to reveal which one I should try next. I'm not forcing my way through God's work; I'm being led by a masterful locksmith that has it all in line.

Seasons

For more than ten years now, I've had plenty of time to think. I'd like to blame it on this writing process, but it's only partially to blame for my analysis paralysis. I mostly sit around and think about all this stuff because I'm very stuck.

I surely can't be the only one that feels stuck even when others would swear I was making progress. Forward motion can look and feel different to every person. I realized I was stuck when I did a Bible study that asked me to analyze my fears. I was holding myself back from a lot of new and exciting and possibly necessary things in life because I was (and still am) afraid. Afraid of what others will think. Afraid of failure. More afraid of success. Afraid of pain. Afraid of being wrong. Afraid of disappointing and of being disappointed. My little brain runs ninety-to-nothing for no reason other than fear.

If I can redeem all the bad things that happen to me, then there is value. If I get to give Jesus glory or bless others in my good days, then there is value in that too. If I grow or become or increase in any way at all, then there is value. But do I really believe that I have value outside of all that effort? What am I worth if I don't work?

For everything there is a season, a time for every activity under heaven. A time to be born and a time to die, a time to plant and a time to harvest. A time to kill and a time to heal, a time to tear down and a time to build up. A time to cry and a time to laugh, a time to grieve and a time to dance. A time to scatter stones and a time to gather stones, a time to embrace and a time to turn away. A time to search and a time to quit searching, a time to keep and a time to throw away. A time to tear and a time to mend, a time to be quiet and a time to speak. A time to love and a time to hate, a time for war and a time for peace.

Ecclesiastes 3:1-8 (NLT)

This set of Scriptures shows that our world works within time. It instructs me to be patient and navigate it well. There are so many things beyond my control, so many things I can't fix or aid or understand. In those instances, I am to rest. The Word of the Lord has promised that things will change. This whole world revolves in seasons. Not just from autumn to spring, but from every other extreme too. Birth and death. Laughter and tears. Love and hate. There is an endless stream of antonyms that could be included in this list; even the passage above seems thorough but incomplete.

No matter what words we'd like to compare and contrast here, the conclusion would be the same: there is a time for both.

In my life, I will experience great joy and deep sorrow. Even within the same day, I can struggle with gains and losses. And you know what, I may not deserve either one. This life is not about earned rewards or unavoidable consequences. As hard as it is to accept, sometimes bad things happen. This is life; it's a fallen nature doing what it does best. There will be great times and there will be terrible times. The remainder of life is frankly the other 90%. Life is about balancing and accepting the extremes. When you receive a blessing beyond your wildest dreams, please be grateful and grow in grace. It keeps you grounded. When the days get long and hard, please allow yourself to grieve what might have been. It helps you persevere.

This is my season and I'm called to live it well. With my uncertainties and my fears and my failures, with my happiness and my hopes and my good intentions. This is now. I'm not told what tomorrow will hold or what Jesus may want to do in the next five years. Frankly, we're not promised anything other than the right now. I really do hope and pray that the next season of my life involves many other things that will make me happy, but if the next season is a little cold and lonely like winter… or if it's a little hot and arid like summer… or if it's beautiful and cozy like fall… or if it's bright and new like spring… my faith cannot waiver and my heart will not change. I'm in this with Jesus for the long haul and I haven't seen all that He has in store.

Chapter Nine

Lesson Four
Believe in the Impossible

Then Jesus said to the disciples, "Have faith in God. I tell you the truth, you can say to this mountain, 'May you be lifted up and thrown into the sea,' and it will happen. But you must really believe it will happen and have no doubt in your heart. I tell you, you can pray for anything, and if you believe that you've received it, it will be yours."

Mark 11:22-24 (NLT)

When God Calls Your Name

I'd like to talk about calling. You know, that weighty and elusive word that we sometimes idolize. Some call it an assignment, others a gift. It can be labeled many things, but the feeling is always the same.

Recovering after the kind of sickness Dad experienced is not guaranteed. Being able to continue life as you once knew it was a surprising gift. After that summer, we could've chosen to spend our time in a million other ways. But we felt called. Called to teach. Called to help. Called to bring forth fruit in a barren wasteland, to sow in the midst of a famine and to reap a harvest. We were called to bring people to a point of decision. Called to strip away the plastic religiosity we've settled for and find the truth of the Word that still has the power to radically change lives. Through it all, we've learned it's as much about what we are called to as what we are called from.

To this he called you through our gospel, so that you may obtain the glory of our Lord Jesus Christ.
2 Thessalonians 2:14 (ESV)

The church has been called to the glory of God. One of my favorite ways to pray asks that each day bring about things for my good and for God's glory. Those are not two separate things. They are single incidents that benefit my life and establish the glory of God on earth. I want my calendar to be full of such things!

Everything God touches has a dual purpose, and we should strive to play right into His plan.

Fight the good fight for the true faith. Hold tightly to the eternal life to which God has called you, which you have declared so well before many witnesses.

1 Timothy 6:12 (NLT)

The Gospel to which we have been called results in eternal life. Sure, this world will hold trials and tribulations, but we're not made for this temporal world alone. We must hold true to the Good News we've received, no matter what comes our way.

Paul, the writer of 1 Timothy, knew his protégé had seen a lot in Ephesus. Timothy knew that life was not all sunshine and roses. He had been hurt, forsaken, lied about and forgotten. Even in those awful times, his persecution and trouble barely compared to his mentor's. These early men of God had a tough row to hoe. With little to go on besides their faith, they had to face crowds and politicians and Pharisees every day. The apostles dared to get out of bed every morning, knowing they would be ridiculed and misunderstood by every friend and neighbor they'd ever had.

In some ways, our faith is no different today. Every believer I know has a story blended with both good and bad circumstances. But in most cases, we've been blessed enough to live in a place that honors our faith. We aren't in danger because of our beliefs, but would our calling change if we were? Are we so sure about our calling that we're willing to stand, or maybe even stand alone?

To do this topic justice and dig even deeper into our calling, we must ask another question. God has saved us for a reason, but He has also saved us from something. If God has called us to eternal life and to partake in His glory, then what must we leave behind?

Don't you realize that those who do wrong will not inherit the Kingdom of God? Don't fool yourselves. Those who indulge in sexual sin, or who worship idols, or commit adultery, or are male prostitutes, or practice homosexuality, or are thieves, or greedy people, or drunkards, or are abusive, or cheat people— none of these will inherit the Kingdom of God. Some of you were once like that. But you were cleansed; you were made holy; you were made right with God by calling on the name of the Lord Jesus Christ and by the Spirit of our God.

1 Corinthians 6:9-11 (NLT)

The list found here has caused so much strife in recent days, but my heart aches because I think we've been focused on all the wrong words. The sins and shortcomings of verses 9 and 10 are common to all flesh. They are all equal. Just like in the other teachings of Jesus, it's about the separation sin has caused and the condition of man's heart. It's not whether being drunk is worse than lying; it's that they both get in the way of God's perfect plan.

Let's focus on the words, "Some of you were once like that." That's the next sentence and something that should be emphasized in my opinion. After analyzing all the pain and problems, what does Paul tell these people? He reminds them that this is not who they are anymore. Upon entering the family of God, we have been cleansed and we have been made right. Being changed changes everything!

If we are called to an unimaginable, eternal glory, then we are also called to leave behind all the former things and pursue with a new and fervent passion everything that God has in store.

One of the other reasons "calling" has such a powerful implication from that summer is that Dad knows he heard the voice of God. We've already discussed what he heard Him say, but let's take a moment to really unpack what it's like when God calls your name.

While still fully medicated and unresponsive, Dad swears his mind was running endlessly. But in one instant, the fog cleared, and he became intensely aware of everything. That's when he heard it. A simple, "Johnny," forever changed his world. This has in turn changed mine.

God speaks. And He knows your name.

That voice would speak several things during Dad's coma, but he knows that it was his name that got his attention. Because of this, we now believe that every heart knows the voice of its Creator. This voice carries with it more than you'll ever know. In one word, you can feel love, care, tenderness and attention. The words are practically dripping with beauty and potential. Just two syllables can wield such priceless truth.

Please let this really sink in. God speaks. And He knows your name.

Stranger to the Covenant

In another one of those fleeting moments, one that would sound a lot like fantasy if I didn't have faith, Dad drifted into enough consciousness to see some bright lights, tubes and IVs. He says it's just a blip of a memory, but in that split second, he didn't feel pain or fear. He simply prayed, "Don't let me die like this."

My father fully believes that he was spared because he asked. He thinks our prayers mattered. He knows that petitioning God's throne affects things, that intercession lets God intervene. We received a miracle that summer, and then God continued to work as we all healed in the years to come. God was present in the moment, but He was present in the process too.

God sees us as special. We are His children, His beloved, the apple of His eye. We are His friends and His family. But we are something else we don't often understand. We are also His covenant partners. God wants to show up in every single believer's life, because while Dad was special, we are not unique.

God has chosen to have a relationship with man. That partnership is governed by covenants. We could write thousands of pages on this topic, but I will try to simplify this theology enough to make my point.

Baker's Evangelical Dictionary of Biblical Theology defines *covenant* as a term "quite commonly used in legal, social (marriage), and religious and theological contexts... [it] is of Latin origin (*con venire*), meaning a coming together. It presupposes two or more parties who come together to make a contract, agreeing on promises, stipulations, privileges, and responsibilities."

The Biblical line of covenants begins with Noah. In Genesis 8, Noah built an altar after the flood waters receded to give praise to the God that sustained them. In acceptance of Noah's sacrifice, God promised to never flood the earth again. The symbol of this covenant is still the rainbow.

Abram, in Genesis 12, established a covenant with God, the One who called him to leave his family and settle in a new land. God promised to bless Abram and his descendants, giving him a new name and promising his family their own nation. In return, Abraham would be faithful to God and he would serve as the channel God used to save the world. The sign of this covenant would be circumcision, proof that God's people were set apart.

When Moses led the children of Israel out of their Egyptian captivity, God updated His covenant with them at Mount Sinai. The Ten Commandments were the basis for this new covenant, but God expounded upon that when He gave Moses the Law. In Exodus 24, we see Moses make a sacrifice to establish this new covenant between God and His people. The Law governed the nation of Israel for thousands of years.

King David understood covenant well. In 1 Samuel 17, when the young boy delivers food to his brothers on the front lines, David asks why the entire army was hiding from the giant. In David's mind, Goliath was an uncircumcised Philistine; he was a stranger to the covenant that had no power over them and no right to their land. It was in that frame of mind that David prepared for the least exciting battle in the Bible.

It seems somewhat fitting that David got to see a new part of the covenant revealed. In 2 Samuel 7, the Lord established David as king to a different throne, the royal line through which the Messiah would come. This promised Son of God would be a descendent of David; He would fulfill the Law, reset everything and basically set the world on fire.

Twenty-eight generations later, a young woman from the line of Nathan and a young man from the line of Solomon would get engaged. An angel would visit them both and the Spirit of the Lord would bless the virgin girl with a son. She would name Him Jesus. He would live like other men, but with unbelievable courage and compassion. He would be charged with blasphemy and die a cruel death on the cross. He would be buried in a borrowed tomb only to defeat death and rise again. His followers would build His church, and He would become the most important figure in history.

While He walked the earth, Jesus Christ did miraculous things. He healed the sick, the lame, the blind, the deaf, the mute and He even raised the dead. He spoke in parables and taught in temples. Wise beyond His years, always humble and holy, He befriended the marginalized and He never once committed a selfish or shameful act. He set the perfect example and then sent the Holy Spirit to help us do the same. His Spirit remains with believers, enabling them to walk in the abundant life Jesus promised.

But now Jesus, our High Priest, has been given a ministry that is far superior to the old priesthood, for he is the one who mediates for us a far better covenant with God, based on better promises. If the first covenant had been faultless, there would have been no need for a second covenant to replace it.

Hebrews 8:6-7 (NLT)

A believer is someone who accepts Jesus Christ as Savior of their souls and Lord of their life. They have become covenant partners with God. This covenant was cut and sealed in the blood of Jesus and it is our hearts that have been marked or circumcised, setting us apart for life with Him. Every time we partake of communion or the Lord's Supper, we are remembering Christ's sacrifice, but we are also establishing His covenant.

Jesus did not perform miracles to show off. He genuinely believed that people shouldn't have to suffer one day longer and that it was an honor to give God glory as He worked and walked with man. God has to know that He's getting the raw end of the deal here. He knows that we are limited, only human flesh and bone. He knows that He is boundless, infinitely divine. And still, He wants this type of relationship with us.

Our relationship is an actual covenant, built on promises, stipulations, privileges, and responsibilities as mentioned above. God promises that He will do all the things we cannot do, and we promise to do all the things He cannot do. His adversary becomes our enemy, while His friends with blessings become our allies with benefits. He has written a whole book about our story; the Bible is full of rules and guidelines and reminders. But every page that has a restriction also has a privilege. God's mercies cannot be escaped. He cannot lie (Titus 1:2). Most of the Pauline epistles challenge us to recognize and consider our responsibilities. God doesn't forcibly require us to do great things in His name, but His Word does encourage us to live up to a new standard. We must admit that He deserves that and so much more.

> *Jesus was sleeping at the back of the boat with his head on a cushion. The disciples woke him up, shouting, "Teacher, don't you care that we're going to drown?" When Jesus woke up, he rebuked the wind and said to the waves, "Silence! Be still!" Suddenly the wind stopped, and there was a great calm. Then he asked them, "Why are you afraid? Do you still have no faith?" The disciples were terrified. "Who is this man?" they asked each other. "Even the wind and waves obey him!"*
>
> *Mark 4:38-41 (NLT)*

Where is our faith? Just like the disciples, we struggle. If we would only ask, I know He would act. If we could only believe, I know He would bring or become exactly what we need. He's empowered me to do fantastic, far-fetched and fabulous things! I fear that I've been waiting on God, but He's been waiting on me. He's offered me everything, the greatest and the grandest, a life beyond anything I could ask or think (Ephesians 3:20). I've settled for what I can see. Even on my best day, I only rally for what I can imagine.

But what if there's more? What if God does dwell in the land of the impossible?

Living and loving like Jesus, exceeding my own expectations, should be a normal part of my everyday life. It takes believing in the impossible to all new heights. Strangers to the covenant no more, the very air surrounding this truth is electric with possibility.

Truly, truly, I say to you, whoever believes in me will also do the works that I do; and greater works than these will he do, because I am going to the Father.

John 14:12 (ESV)

When It Rains

Three days after we got Dad home from the hospital, my mom started feeling sick. She was nauseous, and her left shoulder was aching. It was a Sunday evening and I was out with my friends, chaperoning a youth group event. When I got home late that night, Mom was pacing in the kitchen. I'm so glad I came home earlier than I expected that night, because we packed her up and went to the emergency room just to be safe. After one test, they determined she was having a heart attack and she was rushed into surgery. They put three stents in and determined that she would need three more in a few weeks. Her recovery was so slow. Those nights in the hospital waiting room had taken their toll, but Mom knew that the same God that healed her husband would be more than able to heal her too. With that truth firmly planted in her heart, she became overwhelmed with peace.

Mom's first surgery happened on August 7, 2005. Ideally, her second surgery would be in two months, but she didn't have that many family sick days left. Her doctor performed the second heart surgery around August 25th and Mom went back to work before October 1st. God's providence was as evident here as it had been all summer long. From the perfect surgeon being the only doctor on duty to the attentiveness of a very available hospital staff, nothing regarding Mom's care was a mistake.

I had handled Dad's sickness with more serenity than I ever thought possible. Some of it was the palatable peace of God, but other moments tended toward numbness. If the first of our experiences had stunned me, by this point in our story, I'm in a full daze.

I plodded through life, day after day. September found me graduating college. Life went on. In October, I was ordained six days before I turned twenty-one. Each of these was a momentous life occasion, but all I remember is a blur. I still have no emotion about any of it; I can't recall many details other than what the photographs captured. I thought I was healing, helping myself move on. The truth is though that I was living so far within myself, so emotionally withdrawn, that I was protecting myself from reality. This was the season in which I learned to live in fear. The string of extreme events led to the day I began to fall apart.

November 2005. The day that fell apart became the month I withdrew entirely. I stayed in bed all day, every day. I would eat, I'd listen to music, I'd watch TV, but I didn't want to see anyone, go anywhere or be anything. Physically and emotionally, I had gone as far as I could go. My few days of rest turned into a season of depression. No one blamed me for needing space, but no one also knew the depths to which I was sinking. I know the prayers of my family are what gave me the courage to rejoin my life again. When it came time to prepare for the holidays, I remember thinking I needed to choose. These darker November days were my healing place.

I had to keep showing up so God could keep showing off.

I know that Jesus met each of the people in my family in a unique way that year. Some in sickness, some in stress, and me in silence. We could've made the decision to give up at any time in this story. Choosing to continue may be the hardest decision you have to face some days. I had to keep showing up, so God could keep showing off. I had every right to live in fear. I had every opportunity to give in. But neither of those choices were going to create a story I'd love to tell.

In the years since 2005, I have had at least three other horrific experiences that have thrown me to the foot of the cross. I should live close to Calvary each day, but sadly I forget how precious my life, and His grace, are when things run smoothly. In May 2011, when my grandfather's church was struck by lightning, my family chose to do much of the rebuilding ourselves during the second hottest summer on record. Long days, high temperatures, tight spaces and tons of effort. There are still some days Dad doesn't remember driving home. Why a man that had experienced such a traumatic heat stroke had to do so much manual labor outdoors in a Texas summer, I will never understand. In September 2012, my mom had another heart attack and I contracted E Coli while we were on vacation in Kansas. Lost hotel monies, expensive hospital bills in strange cities and more stress than we knew what to do with made the six-hour drive the longest literal trip of our lives. Most recently in March 2016, I learned CPR from a 9-1-1 operator because my dad had a seizure during an acute sleep apnea episode and was suffocating in his bed at home. A quick response from the paramedics, plus a highly thorough medical team and a heart that had learned a little more about trust, made this experience manageable.

Somewhere in the aftermath of these events, I must admit some nasty truths about myself.

I'm stuck in the doldrums, praying and preparing all while fearful and frenzied. With Dad's last scare, I knew I would have to deal differently. I recognized a lot of unhealthy patterns I had developed. I found many other out-right lies I had started to believe. While it's true what they say, "When it rains, it pours," that's also exactly what rain is supposed to do. That's just what gravity does. I can't get mad when circumstances cannot be avoided or when things just don't meet my expectations. We are supposed to develop a rhythm that can thrive in every season, no matter the tide. Life is supposed to be a crazy blend of amazing and difficult times. I also know that for those in a drought, they pray for the deluge. Maybe we don't know how much we can take or how much we might need.

I have learned that my greatest strength is in my stillness. I have seen God move in miraculous ways because I allowed Him the space to do so. My trust has grown infinitely because I've faced more than a few impossible things and have come through them just fine. All my trials prove that I can't run away. I must expend more energy to find Jesus in those troubled times. I can let my pride and my need to fix all things fall apart, just let it fall short; I'll let it lie in shambles with the rest of my plans and predictions. Anytime someone gives me a piece of bad news, I've learned to sigh in resignation, but then I choose to reply in faith. There's nothing I've seen – and nothing I haven't seen – that Jesus can't lead me through.

The following verses remind me that God is as good as it gets. Sometimes, the only gift He brings is Himself, and in the storm, that is enough.

Blessed is the man who remains steadfast under trial, for when he has stood the test he will receive the crown of life, which God has promised to those who love him... Do not be deceived, my beloved brothers. Every good gift and every perfect gift is from above, coming down from the Father of lights, with whom there is no variation or shadow due to change.

James 1:12, 16-17 (ESV)

Chapter Ten

Lesson Five
Think on These Things

"Finally, brethren, whatever things are true, whatever things are noble, whatever things are just, whatever things are pure, whatever things are lovely, whatever things are of good report, if there is any virtue and if there is anything praiseworthy—meditate on these things."

Philippians 4:8 (NKJV)

If life is doing it's very best to bring us down, it might be time to change the channel. If we can overcome the pessimistic opinions that bombard us, then maybe the noble truths of Scripture can take root. The list of things above from Philippians 4 best describes virtue. Do you have virtue? Have you found the life-giving and delightful moments despite the mundane and the messiness?

What's producing life for you right now? Is it a new book, good music, road trips or cupcakes? No, that might be just for me. Maybe for you, it's quiet times with God and bustling dinner tables with community. We can find true, noble, just, pure and lovely things if we only look. Then when we meditate on these things and give praise despite our pain, that's where we find peace. Verse 9 of the above passage explains that when we practice sowing the Scripture and tending to the truth, then the God of peace will be with us.

We don't have to be perfect to start transforming our lives. Literally anyone can start changing their thoughts at any time, no experience necessary. I can guarantee that life is going to be full of hard work and waiting, but the bountiful harvests are beautiful.

Displaced and Longing for Home

We all felt a bit lost when we were living at the hospital. No matter how many times you go through situations like this or how skilled you know the nurses are, it's never easy to leave a loved one. Mom and Mawmaw toughed it out. It was a just-in-case thing; we didn't want to leave because we hadn't given up hope.

So, they slept on beds made of coffee tables and office chairs. They ate in shifts. They only went home to shower and change when another family member could be present to wait. It was their own version of camping, always without the s'mores to make it worth it. It was rough, but they were very determined.

During this time, I could've stayed home alone each night, but we all decided that probably wasn't best. My Aunt Roxie, who is also technically my next-door neighbor, let me sleep at her house throughout this whole affair. It was comfortable and nice; sharing meals and relaxing with music or TV helped get my mind off reality. My family's presence and hospitality helped me cope in so many ways. Life is always easier with a good community, remember that.

But in hindsight, I realize one great spiritual lesson I overlooked while living it. No matter how great it was, it wasn't home. For all its amazing qualities, it wasn't where I belonged. Some things felt right, and we could've made it work for longer than we had to, but there was no denying that it only worked for a short season. Let's be honest, I was displaced, staying some place good, but some place wrong.

Circumstances tend to displace people. After spending the last few years working in disaster relief, I can tell when someone is longing to go back to the familiar. It's inconceivable to lose everything you've ever known, so being displaced is as much an emotional perspective as it is a physical place. If you are displaced, you are longing for home. Things won't be right again until you feel that sense of belonging. Many will even settle for a semblance of home. If it's music or a certain type of food, there is something happy about the stability.

I needed to be at my aunt's, but it wasn't home. Mom wasn't going to leave the hospital, but it wasn't home. Dad was fighting the battle of his life, but he still wasn't home. We each had to be somewhere we didn't quite fit. We did the best we could in the middle of the situation, but now we see just how different everything was. There was confusion and sadness; at other times, we all felt very, very lost. When you end up somewhere you don't belong, you must fully trust God and commit everything to Him. Only He could turn being stuck in an awkward place into progress and forward motion.

I now see how this impacts my life today. Every day, I must be somewhere I don't belong. The old song says, "This world is not my home, I'm just a'passing through." As a child of God, my soul should be longing for something it cannot currently obtain. I should be letting my hospital experience teach me this in a profound way. Just like with our sleeping arrangements during that time, we must follow and trust. We make the best of bad situations. We follow God intently. We have to do what we feel called to do, but we can never forget the end goal of all of our efforts and we must never get too comfortable here.

In the wilderness experience of Scripture, the Israelites longed to be free from Egypt. But once their journey started, they lost sight of everything ahead of them and many in the tribes did nothing but murmur and complain about how miserable they felt. Some even wanted to return to slavery because it seemed safer. They had their friends and families. God had led them out of Egypt with a mighty hand. They feasted at a manna buffet each morning and then sweet water would pour from rocks along their path if they needed it. Millions of people experienced the magnificent work of God every day and totally missed the point of the journey.

Even after learning a wilderness lesson, the nation of Israel would fall back into the trap of comfort many more times. When wanting a king, when trying to evade Babylon, when trapped in captivity – time and again, the nation was always looking for a way to solve their own problems or to increase their comfort instead of trusting and obeying the God that had led them through. Life would become too tough, they'd lose their focus and then would want to quit.

We must let our longing lead us closer to Him.

We are presented with that option daily. The flesh part of all mankind is drawn back to the familiar territory of temptation and the anguish of guilt and shame. Every sinful tendency we have reminds us that we are separated from God and His perfect ways. That's displacement. But to redeem our separation, we must allow our displacement to become a longing for something greater.

When we are displaced and longing for home, we cannot afford to seek comfort in our abilities or knowledge alone. We cannot forget the eternal price on every decision. No amount of understanding today is worth losing sight of God's plan and purpose for tomorrow. We must let our longing lead us closer to Him. In our flesh, it becomes very easy to seek answers and not truth. It's even easier to settle for a semblance of what we were created for.

In this life, we will never be fully satisfied. If we are doing this Christianity thing right, we will always be looking for more. We are not home yet. Sleep on that cozy bed. Rest and grow and learn and do. Persevere. Rejoice. In the end, realize God's worked on your behalf at every turn and remember that the sorrow here doesn't compare to the glory that follows. Don't be afraid to seek, long, knock or ask. Keep searching and looking for the only thing that fits like it should – an intimate, loving relationship with Jesus, the only One that understands. Let Him be the guide; let Him lead you home.

Unlikely, But Not Unworthy

We weren't strong enough. Right in the middle of our hospital wilderness, we were confused and hanging on by one thread alone, our faith. I remember lots of sleepless nights and long, exhausting days. God has done an incredible work redeeming the time. Since I've had plenty of time to process the experience, I am now certain the hospital season was much more profound than I've ever realized.

Today, I thought about how unlikely of a people we are. First with my family and then with mankind in general. It's humbling and a little bit crazy that God wants to keep us around.

My family is awesome. I'm beyond blessed to have this many God-fearing, Christ-following loved ones around me. Our situation has always been unique. We live close to each other and are highly involved in each other's lives. God uses our close relationships to benefit the kingdom quite often. Whether it's donating items, volunteering time, or singing, preaching and playing; you can usually find us serving Jesus together. It's a wild journey, but we don't really know how to go it alone.

If we were an unlikely crew before our wilderness experience, we are even more unlikely now. Before, we were so sure about everything, but now we are much more honest and vulnerable. Once afraid of our broken incompleteness, we now rest in our inabilities and are actually comfortable without all the answers. When we thought our gifts and talents would take us somewhere special, now we see that we are nothing outside of God's bigger plan and we are totally committed to His vision. Instead of reasoning the situation away, I came to terms with it and believe that we are now responsible to do and be something great. Someone once told us that God was a good investor, so I want to make sure all His efforts count.

We aren't the best at any one thing; in fact, some say that our stubborn stick-to-itiveness is our best trait. We've learned to be trustworthy people of character, the kind of people that have more integrity than they have sense. All these things are usable by God and they were some of the first things He worked on in our lives. And since we've submitted to be usable, we're presented with opportunities to serve Him daily in this way.

Scripture is full of these unlikely people too, so we're in great company. I can also assume that if you've been a person of faith for any length of time, then you probably see a bit of unlikeliness in yourself. When Jesus came to this world in human form, He was surrounded by people with questionable pasts and even more indiscernible futures – tax collectors, prostitutes, thieves, businessmen, family members, Pharisees and friends. The stories Jesus dared to write in their lives should inspire us to embrace our uniqueness. Forget shying away from a calling because of fear or concern! Realize that your worst behavior or your most despised decision is nothing but untapped greatness in the hands of God.

The enemy that we fight wants to tell us that all our negative traits make us unworthy, that in all our mistakes we must've missed God. While it's true that we could never have earned the gifts of God, the Scripture makes sure to point out at multiple times that God did all the effort when we could not. God acted from His love. If I had to rely on my abilities alone, I'd never measure up. But because I've turned to Him and forsaken myself, then anything within His realm is possible.

And we can see that it was while we were powerless to help ourselves that Christ died for sinful men. In human experience it is a rare thing for one man to give his life for another, even if the latter be a good man, though there have been a few who have had the courage to do it. Yet the proof of God's amazing love is this: that it was while we were sinners that Christ died for us.

Romans 5:6-8 (PHILLIPS)

Knowing how far we had fallen, foreseeing all the sin that had tripped us up, the Son of God came to earth to redeem and restore us. He gave His entire life to fix our broken relationship. He did all the work when I was incapable of anything. In the most astonishing, selfless act history has ever seen, Jesus died for all mankind and offered His life in exchange for mine. His life in exchange for yours. His life in exchange for us all. Every penalty I deserved and every sin that weighed me down – GONE! I am not worthy because I'm smart, pretty, talented or different in some way. I am worthy because my Creator declared me so. In an act of His Word, just like in those of creation, He spoke and my whole identity changed.

I am not worthy because I'm smart, pretty, talented or different in some way. I am worthy because my Creator declared me so.

So, when we battle unworthiness, we can reference a new reality. When we feel distant and undeserving, we must remember that we're not accepted because we're good. My father was not healed because of anything he had done. My family is not blessed by our merit. We made sure our prayers were unhindered; we gave ourselves fully over to the plan of God and trusted that He would see us through. But when we received the answer we had diligently sought, we rejoiced and gave God the glory. Still today, it's about the Giver and not about the gifts.

We are unlikely candidates to carry a testimony like this. I worry we'll screw it up all the time. But in the end, I'm asked to bear this story proudly and always be willing to give an account of what the Lord has done. I'm unlikely, but not unworthy. I didn't have to earn a spot on this team; I was in good with the coach. He is my Creator and He knows me best.

Who Needs Commandments

I absolutely love the God we serve. I desperately want the world to see a difference between the new me and the old me. Most people see changes when believers forsake their bondage in sin to find new life in Christ, but my life should also be drastically different when I step from simple faith into deep trust. Without my summer in the wilderness, I might not know the difference. To me, faith is the internal belief that God exists and that He is who He says He is. Fueled by ideas, answers, testimonies and truth, it's a head knowledge that leads to a heart change. But trust is letting God be all He is, with no explanation or reason why. Faith likes its evidence; it may be all the proof I need at the time, but it brings about a fruitful conclusion, something that is real and tangible. Trust requires me to let God work when I think I could handle things on my own; it could also ask me to act as if the answer is here while it's still on its way. True trust doesn't need a reason at all.

When I woke up in the middle of a story I didn't want to be living, my faith didn't waver. I had enough experience with Jesus to know that He was right there all the time. My trust however was non-existent. In its place, there was fear and anger. I wanted to be in charge and to be able to fix things so badly. Loving me through that rotten attitude, Jesus taught me an awful lot in those dim days. I had never trusted Him, but I was ready to accept that invitation.

The characteristics of Christ that can now mark my life are earth shattering. Other than the core personality traits and my physical appearance, everything else has changed. Priorities, sense of humor, attitude, relationships, perspective — God left no stone unturned when He started rooting out evil and planting His seeds of hope in my life. If I was going to trust Him, I would have to be different. No longer in charge of my destiny, I was now willing to give up control.

Living up to the higher standard defined by a relationship with God is rarely fun, but the rewards outshine even the brightest human accolade. Choosing to live above reproach and shunning worldly desires in favor of God is not the simple, easy choice most days. Over time, the desires of the flesh fade and the longing to please God grows, but my human nature is ever present. The attacks of the enemy may look different now, but they are still there. Temptation follows even the strong; your focus and dedication because of God's love must be more powerful than any outside influence.

When I fully understood the significance of my dedication to God, I was able to love Him more dearly and follow Him more freely. It was like a switch in my brain. My love for my sin and my previous life vanished when I realized why I must live up to my potential in Christ. You see, God loves us. That's the simple Gospel message. John 3:16 makes it clear. He loves, He gave, we live. But along the way, we've forgotten to emphasize the importance of a deeper relationship with the Lord. Not knowing about Him, not seeing Him at work around us, not just believing that He exists... but falling madly, irrevocably, passionately and crazily in love with Him. Like infatuated lovers who believe the world cannot revolve without their partner, I think that's the kind of love we're supposed to find in God. Only that love can birth trust. Anything less and I would still be living in fear.

Here is the point: my life is different because I am dedicated to the one I love. Why shun sin? Why make the daily difficult choice to change? Why try so hard to please God all the time? Most people look at my behaviors and the most common answer is that I'm just a legalist. I don't drink, I don't smoke, I don't sleep around, I don't do drugs. They observe and wonder, "Well, what are you allowed to do?" I'll be the first to admit that I do follow a set of rules. There is a list of things I won't do, places I won't go, and words I won't say. But I am not restrained by those laws or any others found in Scripture; I am constrained by an unexplainable love. (2 Corinthians 5:14 KJV)

The only One that loves me more than life itself has asked me to be more like Him. The Creator of my universe and the Son of my sky has requested that I put Him above all else. I do not obey, cower, listen or move out of fear. I respond out of an undying love for my Savior and my God. I need not fear death, pain or even hell. I am compelled to obey out of sheer gratitude, amazement and delight. Who needs commandments when you have a commitment?

The Law given in the Old Testament revealed just how far sin separated us from God, but it's told that the Law wasn't God's first choice. In fact, it seems that the Lord would've preferred a closer walk with man and daily fellowship from the beginning. If the Israelite nation would've sought the Lord daily and responded in faith, there would be no need for a huge chunk of Biblical history. After the death, burial and resurrection of Jesus; that closer relationship was possible and the Holy Spirit dwelling inside of believers finally allowed us to recognize our capabilities. Sin still hinders but the possibilities are limitless. Being drawn to God, trusting Him with literally every step and outcome of our life, is the greatest goal we could ever have.

Living in the balanced rhythm of goodness and grace is not the easy way; there are ditches on both sides of the righteous road, so truth is not always easy to find. My seasons of legalism were also my seasons of distrust. I was doing all the right things for all the wrong reasons. I've seen what self-righteousness can do first-hand. What's worse is I've seen what fear, guilt, condemnation and judgment can do too. Whether convincing ourselves we are good enough or telling others they aren't, we're operating in a role that was never ours to play. Even though Scripture says there is no condemnation for those in Christ Jesus, Christian society has made sure that there was plenty of condemnation for those that fell short of the expectations of the church.

I'm not sure I can ever repair all the damage done, but there is true freedom to be found in the Lord. To promote the backwards kingdom of Christ, one must use both words and deeds. I can't let people continue to believe the lies that are promoted. Our testimonies tell the truth! Those that ask about God's work in my life and why I have the behaviors I do often find that I have something much more compelling than religion. I'm constantly on my guard to make sure that I haven't saddled a high horse; I'm not afraid to put my pride in its place. I am no better than any other person because I hear and obey God. I could, however, be happier than other people because I've found my purpose. I can live with great hope, fully trusting and relying on Christ, because I've found my one true Love.

Because you're probably wondering and because I've been asked more times than I can count, I'd like to at least mention that you've been reading my list of "rules" for several chapters now. Each lesson or chapter in this book has laid my faith's foundation so you can skim the Table of Contents to get a better idea.

Ultimately, the only rule is that He leads, and I follow. The enumerated list just helps define some boundaries; it gives me a good starting point and quickly brings things to my remembrance. I know these principles are the best way to judge all my decisions and disciplines. There are millions of right ways to serve the Lord, because He writes every story uniquely. Your list can be shorter, longer or non-existent. Thinking like this and even being open to the Jesus's edits are just the best way for me to rely, remind and revive. My standard is achievable, but still impossible without a renewed mind and the regenerating work of the Holy Spirit. I don't work to earn my salvation or to find more grace; the reward of dedication and obedience is the relationship I've created with God Himself. I love Him. I trust Him. I follow Him. But I'll never forget that He first loved me (1 John 4:19).

Chapter Eleven

Lesson Six
Bear Fruit

"But the fruit of the Spirit is love, joy, peace, patience, kindness, goodness, faithfulness, gentleness, self-control; against such things there is no law. And those who belong to Christ Jesus have crucified the flesh with its passions and desires. If we live by the Spirit, let us also keep in step with the Spirit."

Galatians 5:22-25 (NASB)

My faith in the Lord is strong. But if my faith cannot be moved, then why do I still experience so much frustration? How was I supposed to cope with all the pain and lack? How could I prepare for what's next when I never saw this coming? Why had I become so fearful? I knew for the first time that something was missing. I saw through all these circumstances that my trust could be bought. No matter what I believed, I could never find the rest I was so desperately seeking without fully surrendering to God.

I kept praying for answers, trying to build a dependence on God but never really coming close. I see now that so much of my effort was spent praying for things that God has already paid for, provided and given freely to me. I didn't need to waste my time searching for God's peace; that was a fruit of the Spirit and I could have it present and working in my life daily. Sure, I'd have to learn how to follow His promptings and more fully give into His plan, but God could not give me any more peace than He already had. Joy – I didn't have to be waiting around for a special delivery. Patience, same thing. I didn't want to pray for that anyway, so it's great that it's already here.

These attributes can be evident in our life every single day. Because of grace and the redemptive work of the cross, we can have a close, intimate relationship with God. In that exchange, we also receive the Holy Spirit. He is living in us, working God's purposes out in our normal lives. I believe that when good things happen, He is to blame. The fruit of the Spirit can take root and overtake my heart because my faith has grown into trust.

Building Something that Lasts

I learned very quickly that my faith must always be ready, constant in season and out. I couldn't have read enough Scripture during these forty days to prepare me for such an experience. There isn't time to build a foundation when a city is under siege. The things that get you through the tough times have been sown and cultivated during the good days. You must have that history to rely on. I don't know how to survive if I don't know Jesus, but I only know Him by spending time, listening and learning at His feet. It takes time to know Him, but a crisis can happen overnight.

My grandmother, Sister Young, had the best faith. Notice that I don't say the most, because it's never been about a size or an amount. It's all about fidelity, strength and resilience. I'd rather hitch the trailer of my life to a faith that has seen a thing or two than to try and trust in a faith that's bright, shiny and new.

Mom's mom knew life and it's struggle a little too well. Being widowed for more than twenty years, losing a teenage son in a car accident in 1959, being a pastor's wife in more than a few small towns - her faith had seen its fair share of trials. But her faith is what made her the best prayer warrior, the most wonderful woman of God. It was her survival that had made her strong. After she passed away, we found this written in her handwriting on the last page of her Bible:

The way is not hard with my Savior
The road has already been trod.
God will walk so close beside me,
And I will be led by the Son of God.

See, it's the turbulence that reveals how skilled the Captain is. It's the rough seas that make us appreciate the calm and serene shore. One of the quotes that has seen me through my most recent difficult time is, "A ship in harbor is safe, but that is not what ships are built for." It's about a faith that's been weathered and worn, one that will see you through absolutely anything you could face.

I don't know where I'd be without my grandmother's prayers during the summer of 2005. When we admitted Dad to the hospital on that Friday, she sat in the waiting room and prayed out loud for hours. Out. Loud. Not in a timid voice that petitioned God with fear and trembling. No, she argued with God, boldly at times. Reminding Him of His promises and everything He had said. Quoting Scripture and weaving in and out of her prayer language, the behavior earned us some funny looks. But she never cared.

Even years later when thinking about that day, she never apologized. Her faith had taught her that there was a time to be silent, but there was also a time to be vocal and tenacious.

Instead, you must worship Christ as Lord of your life. And if someone asks about your Christian hope, always be ready to explain it.

1 Peter 3:15 (NLT)

When we were coming out of this wilderness, most people asked how we were able to stay positive. When the doctors would give us grave news and no hope, no one knew how we were able to respond calmly. We needed an answer that meant something, but sometimes faith is hard to put into words. My family learned to simply nod, smile and give all the credit to our faith. We did not go through this trial to no avail; we came out of this experience with a testimony stronger than any demon in hell.

It took standing on promises we had almost forgotten. It took praying the Word when all you wanted to do was cry. It took being honest with yourself and others, trusting God with all the sleepless nights and weary days. It took speaking words of life when all you saw was death. It took screaming at the ceiling and sitting in the silence. It took everything we had and even more we weren't sure we could muster.

In that day and in that time, life had stopped. The only thing we had to go on was what we had already established. This is the challenge of the now. What am I doing today that will withstand something tomorrow?

Experiences and Arguments

Recovery gave us more than enough time to think. One of the things we'd often do is talk with Dad about what had happened during those twenty-eight days he was in a coma. He wanted to know what the doctors had said, how we reacted, what we kept doing or changed, who had come to visit, what was new or different. Every time we'd talk about one of the friends or family that had come by, Dad would want to call and talk to them. He'd just touch base, to thank them for standing with his family and just to prove that things were getting better. You can tell people that you're recovering, but they may not believe you until they see it for themselves.

One day, we called an old associate pastor. He and his son had come to visit because they heard about our circumstances. We hadn't caught up in almost six years by that point, but the time and distance faded away and we were able to be a part of each other's stories again. Dad also called his old Sunday school teacher, a dear friend that had been a part of our family for almost sixty years. She and her associate pastor (whom we also dearly love) came to visit more than once. They continued to lift us up in prayer and were there if we needed anything. Several families that had once attended our church but had left for a variety of reasons also dropped by. Some even came back into our lives after long, strained absences. I'll always believe that was part of God's redemptive plan. Friends from all across North Texas came by to talk and pray. But we had one encounter we will never forget.

If you're familiar with the Collin County area or have been here very long, there's a good chance you know a Hooper. While some members of the family have been more infamous than important, we run into people all the time that we know or people who have heard about us. My grandma taught me early on that my reputation would precede me. I look like my Daddy and talk like my Daddy. With his curly hair and his last name, there'd be no mistaking who I belonged to. When I left my house, I was representing my entire heritage. This was something I never took lightly, but something I've only recently come to appreciate.

I say all of this to explain that we have cousins and uncles and other relatives that have pastored and worked in churches all over North Texas too. Even when I'm filing paperwork with the county clerk, she'll ask, "Are you related to those Hoopers?" She usually means something great, like a pastor or a friend that positively impacted her life, so it's easy to be proud of who we are and what we come from.

One such family member was our Uncle Butch. Technically, he would've been my third cousin, but you know how all those lines get blurred. He pastored the church my family attended before we started our own. In 1979, three weeks after my mom and dad married, my dad felt like he was supposed to travel with Uncle Butch to North Carolina for a string of tent revivals. It was on that trip in the fall of '79 that Dad decided he was called to something a little different than farming. Just like when Jesus called some ship workers to become fishers of men, God had started calling our family to sow a different kind of seed in a more eternal kind of soil.

So, Dad and Uncle Butch go way back; he was a consistent positive influence in our lives whether we saw much of each other or not. Uncle Butch and several people from his family came to visit Dad in the hospital, so when we were making our thank-you phone calls mentioned above, Dad was happy to call him that day.

After catching up for a little while, Uncle Butch told Dad something we've never forgotten. To be honest, it still shapes our life. We rediscovered who we are and what our purpose could be because Uncle Butch said these words: "A man with an experience is worth ten with an argument."

All the Bible study in the world cannot make up for one real experience with Jesus. The kind of time that marks a man's life cannot just be studied or considered; the most life-changing things must be walked out with great discipline and humility.

> All the Bible study in the world cannot make up for one real experience with Jesus.

We didn't have to argue with anyone ever again. You don't have to believe me or even agree with my theology; I've seen too much for you to change my mind. I'm not proud or close-minded, just experienced. There's an old Gospel song that says, "I was there when it happened, so I guess I oughta know." And that's the truth. It doesn't mean you're perfect; it doesn't mean life is always pretty. It means that you're sure about who and where and what you are in Jesus.

We will leave a great legacy of faith behind. When people around here remember us, this is what I want them to know. This family was built on faith alone. We weathered unimaginable storms, faced unexplainable loss, trod unattainable ground. Even back to the days of my great, great-grandpa, we were no stranger to both the trials of life and the good grace of God. We have a strong testimony and we're becoming less afraid to share it every day. What God will do with all of this has yet to be seen, but we will be here to be involved when the purpose is more fully revealed.

I don't know if I could ever properly thank the people that helped us along the way. In fact, I'm not sure Uncle Butch knew just how drastically he impacted our home. I will forever believe that we recovered in a more complete way because of his shared truth. We now also sow that idea into each life we touch; go, experience God, and don't be afraid to tell your story. May we all learn to live our testimonies proudly.

> *And they overcame him because of the blood of the Lamb and because of the word of their testimony, and they did not love their life even when faced with death.*
>
> *Revelation 12:11 (NASB)*

Never Mine to Carry

How much of what weighs me down was never mine to carry?

If you know me, you probably also know that I have an extremely heightened sense of responsibility. I take things personally and get deeply involved even in things that are not my business. This is a quality leadership trait that becomes my weakness. I'm a fixer and I seem to purposefully surround myself with people that need help.

After our summer in the hospital, my dad promised our entire family that he would slowly reintegrate back into society. He wouldn't jump in and do too much too soon; he promised to take his time and calculate just how much stress he was putting himself under each day. We became quite picky about each decision and tried to never be over-committed. When you have no idea what made you sick, you don't know how to react. You tend to avoid everything out of fear, but that can only be the answer for so long. If we wanted our electricity to stay on that summer, someone was going to have to get back to work and make it happen.

I started worrying about everything that was once in Dad's domain. I chose to add his recovery, our ever-growing list of medical bills, and all his waiting sound system clients to my to-do list. I was already processing portfolio reviews and job searches because I was in my senior-level classes at art school. I had been handling our daily books and bills for several months before Dad's sickness, so there was management for that too. Lawyers, CPAs, property taxes and doctors were all piled on my plate. Here is where I will try to justify all of this as me being mature and responsible. I was helping my family by carrying a lot of this weight. But let's be honest, I refused help from people that were willing to assist me, and I never once asked Jesus if any of this new stuff was really mine to carry.

Just admitting that paragraph above is a little rough on my ego. Acting like I've got everything under control is my greatest temptation; I've been deceived for years into thinking that I've fooled everyone. Only recently did I learn that everyone knows I don't have it all together.

The women in my family have given me incredible examples to follow. Now that I know it's perfectly acceptable to be messy and learning and honest, I can see that these traits marked their lives too. It also makes their idiosyncrasies make a little more sense.

Grandmomma's favorite song to hum at any down time of the day was "Leave It There." I don't really remember her singing it any during our time at the hospital; it was just more of a constant with her. Because she believed the truth of this hymn, this simple tune helps me live my life.

If the world from you withholds of its silver and its gold,
And you must get along on meager fare,
Just remember in His word how He feeds the little birds,
Take your burden to the Lord, leave it there.

Leave it there, leave it there.
Take all your burdens to the Lord and leave them there.
If you trust Him through your doubt,
He will surely lead you out.
Take your burden to the Lord and leave it there.

Every single weight that I carry was never meant to be bore alone. There is a place for all my problems at the foot of the cross. I've known from a very early age that I should approach God with all these burdens, so I feel like I cast all my cares over to Him rather easily. I however have a habit of picking it all back up. Even after confession and forgiveness, I still feel like these are my problems to bear. I can't just leave them with my caring Savior; I must try to prove myself and my worth by trudging through the pain alone. I also feel like I must complain about it just to let everyone know how much I've had to sacrifice. This pattern stunts my growth and hinders any chance I have at walking out my repentance, but it's a result I revert to so often. I must ask myself, "If I can't hand over the non-essentials, then do I really trust God with my eternity?"

Hebrews 12:1-2 encourages the believer to lay aside the sin and the weights that so easily entangle us. Our goal should be to run this race with patience and fervor, finding freedom in the finished work of Christ. He endured inconceivable amounts of pain just so that you and I may overcome weariness and discouragement. He came to save us from all sin and darkness, but He also cares deeply about the things we walk through every day and how we respond to each circumstance.

The foot of the cross is sacred ground. It's a divine place where my best days and my worst days couldn't add up to enough. But in the blood and in the final work of Jesus, I can be declared righteous, justified and saved. His one sacrifice covered all my sin and shame; when I could never be enough, He did all the work for me. I can't earn it or deserve it. Grace is just about the most unfair thing we can experience. But it is love. It's beautiful and miraculous and transformational. You can't leave the foot of the cross unchanged. So, if I'm different after experiencing God, then the load that I carry should be different too.

Grace is just about the most unfair thing we can experience. But it is love.

Then Jesus said, "Come to me, all of you who are weary and carry heavy burdens, and I will give you rest. Take my yoke upon you. Let me teach you, because I am humble and gentle at heart, and you will find rest for your souls. For my yoke is easy to bear, and the burden I give you is light."

Matthew 11:28-30 (NLT)

After Jesus touches our lives, the burdens we bear should be light. My sense of responsibility should be present in my life; other people should know that they can trust me. Being responsible is a good thing, but being consumed by that responsibility is suffocating. There is a balance between taking on things I was never meant to carry and flippantly avoiding things that should be my concern. This is where wisdom and the Holy Spirit meet me. I didn't just drop everything when I realized I was doing too much, and I was trying to earn my salvation and people's respect. I consciously reviewed aspects of my life and I began to let things go. Even if I still needed to oversee the situation in some way, I didn't have to take it so personally and its effect on my everyday life needn't be so profound. I now know my calling and I'm trying to stay in my lane. I pick up what is mine to move forward with, but I'm trying to walk with Jesus and let Him carry more. I'm going to make it up this mountain, but I won't be trying to make it alone.

Chapter Twelve

Lesson Seven
Trust the Lord, Not the Heart

"Blessed is the man who trusts in the Lord, whose trust is the Lord. He is like a tree planted by water, that sends out its roots by the stream, and does not fear when heat comes, for its leaves remain green, and is not anxious in the year of drought, for it does not cease to bear fruit. The heart is deceitful above all things, and desperately sick; who can understand it?"

Jeremiah 17:7-9 (ESV)

Land Mines

You can never over-emphasize the lessons you take away from life-altering experiences. It was one thing to learn, but it's another thing to share. One of the analogies my family left the hospital with involved land mines.

On the surface, the simple lesson we must learn is this: when you don't know where to tread, you must stand still. At times, it's appropriate to retrace your steps and back out of a bad situation, but usually the only way through it is to pause, assess, regroup and wait. We can be in more danger if we are in a hurry than if we were to just take our time, listen and obey.

Waiting, pausing, listening… these are not natural responses to fear. It's easier to run; I would prefer to overreact. But safety is only found in the waiting. But what is it that we're waiting for?

I have read all the Scriptures about waiting and I have a whole Pinterest board dedicated to quotes on the subject. The pretty landscapes and cursive writing do little to calm my nerves, but the truth contained in the Scriptures has always had a positive effect.

It is the Lord Who goes before you; He will [march] with you; He will not fail you or let you go or forsake you; [let there be no cowardice or flinching, but] fear not, neither become broken [in spirit—depressed, dismayed, and unnerved with alarm].

Deuteronomy 31:8 (AMP)

Envision this: A field of battle, an army moving and progressing towards the enemy's camp. Marching in formation, one knit unit, a perfectly tight group, all-for-one and one-for-all. But someone makes a wrong move and an explosion ripples through the air. You're unsure of who was hurt, where to go, what to do. What is your expert, trained reaction? You do nothing. In this scene, this is where I see the verse from Deuteronomy take full effect.

It is the Lord that is with us. When bad things happen, or circumstances take us by surprise, we are not alone. The smoke may need to clear, and we might need to regain our senses, but when we're able to see and think, we will notice Him. He is marching with us and He won't leave – not in the good and NEVER in the bad. Do not flinch. Do not fear. Do not even become disheartened.

In conjunction with this idea, the Lord recently gave me a new revelation about all this waiting. In almost every situation, waiting on God requires discipline, diligence and determination. The Lord told me that no matter what it is I'm waiting on, I must remember that I'm waiting on Him. I'm not waiting on the object of my desire. I'm not waiting on the job or the husband or more money. I'm waiting on Him and He will take good care of me.

In the middle of the battlefield of life, every step is a risk. All the people, places and things that consume our day could very easily lead us astray. When I think I'm following Jesus, but things go wrong, I now pause and wait until I can discern everything with wisdom. If I don't have God's peace, then I don't move. There's too much at stake. There're too many eternal consequences for me not to tread lightly. Every moment of the day is an opportunity, and after a hospitalized wilderness experience, we take nothing for granted.

I'm not waiting on the object of my desire. I'm not waiting on the job or the husband or more money. I'm waiting on Him... and He will take good care of me.

For months after the summer of 2005, while everyone in the family was recovering in their own way, we really took this land mine vision to heart. We did not commit to anything without a clear sign from the Lord. Over time, we grew comfortable again with our own ideas and our plan, allowing ourselves to interpret the minimal information God had provided. Going my own way increases the danger exponentially in my life. Even with the best of intentions, the potential for bad situations is multiplied. It is always during the messes I have made for myself that I remember God's instructions best.

The challenge is to review without running away or reacting hastily. The goal is prayer, to simply communicate with Jesus all the time. While my tendency is to say, "Thanks, I've got it from here," you won't find me saying or believing that much anymore.

Now, you can find me constantly in the quiet places, trying to hear the plan and the purpose. My entire life is still full of land mines, but the Captain of Hosts has a map for the way out. My soul is still safely in His care. I'm placing my little feet in His big boot prints and we are marching on – to beauty, in rhythm, to glory.

Trust Is a Choice

In the last chapter, we discussed how our lives can be marked by the fruit of the Spirit. The best fruit comes from a life of trust. In addition to the list of fruit in Galatians 5, there are even better things for us to bear.

But now that you have been set free from sin and have become slaves of God, the fruit you get leads to sanctification and its end, eternal life.

Romans 6:22 (ESV)

The other fruit we can bear because we are the children of God includes holiness, sanctification and eternal life. These are all things that should be evident in our life. Honestly, they should be a by-product of our reliance and dependence upon God. We shouldn't spend years of our time trying to ask for or perfect them. They are the natural side effects of His working. Living unto God should make us unmistakably His, marked by His character and set apart for His purposes.

The reason we struggle to see these traits develop is that they all require something more than faith. Trust would be the best word to describe what most Christians are missing. The fidelity, the purpose, the strength. There are some things only available to those who are willing to dig deep and do the hard work of believing. If you signed up to follow Jesus because someone told you it was easy, then I hope you're ready for a wild ride. This life is beautiful and complex and incredible, but I'd never label it as easy.

Trust is a choice. Trust cannot just happen to us. While many things within the realm of serving God can be passive and occur without all our effort, choosing to trust is not one of them. Trust is the vital choice we must make when confronted with a crisis of faith. We can believe God is good and that He can do great things, but if we do not trust Him to do so, then we still try to remain in control of our lives. Tying up our destiny to things only within our control is a perilous thing. Trying to serve God while making yourself master of your affairs can only end in heartache and loss.

The psalms are filled with David's songs and poetry. True to his life, his faith in God was built on experiences, both great and small. He had battled giants, lost children, been crowned king and brought back from the brink more than once. Yet he says time and again, "Trust." (See Psalm 27, 34, 56, 62, and 71 for some of my favorite examples)

I hope that I remember all this the next time I go through a wilderness experience. I pray that every situation brings me to my knees, or even to my end, where the Lord can work with my brokenness to restore and reconcile me to His plan. I could save myself so much worry by prioritizing my trust as much as I do my faith. I want my beliefs to naturally birth a reliance on God. He doesn't forget or forsake us. He can't harm us, and His love abounds with new mercies every day. He can be believed, but He can also be trusted. In all the situations I face, He deserves my unwavering devotion. He's worthy of my everything. I've spent years striving and searching and seeking. Now, I'm going to give Him my trust and see where He can go from there.

May the God of hope fill you with all joy and peace as you trust in him, so that you may overflow with hope by the power of the Holy Spirit.

Romans 15:13 (NIV)

Hollywood's White Horse

Hollywood has not prepared me for reality. Our culture has gotten my hopes up and I have not managed my expectations very well. Normally, I discuss this in conjunction with high school, relationships and home life. While all of that is still true, I pause here to think about it in a different way.

For our extended hospital stay, there were so many situations I was unprepared for. I didn't have a quirky, best-friend sidekick to help me through the hard times. There was never a music montage that seamlessly blended the monotonous hours together. I didn't end up falling in love with another patient or doctor; no white knight came riding to my rescue in the waiting room. I couldn't follow the wise advice of inanimate objects or the oldest ladies in town. Basically, in hindsight, if I believed in Hollywood alone, I'd be extremely disappointed.

Growing up, you watch Disney and dress like princesses. Magic awaits around every corner, children are wide-eyed, and bright stars light up every dark sky. In the movies, life may hit hard times, but you always know that everyone (except the bad guy) will bounce back in less than ninety minutes. All questions have answers and we can all find a happily ever after. When reality catches up to you, you must learn to manage expectations. If you're still expecting everything to work out like a predictable plot, then no conclusion will ever feel right. However, if you're looking for growth, progress and change, then I can guarantee you'll love the outcome.

That is what has made me fall in love with my story. I quit looking for all kinds of other answers and began to accept what was right before me. When you genuinely look at what surrounds you, you can still experience breathtaking types of magic. Everyday miracles are just as wondrous as anything Hollywood could offer, but this life of mine is real and can impact so many others.

I've spent so much time waiting on all the wrong things. Frankly, I've recently learned that I can't be surrendered to Jesus and awaiting my American dream. Those two ideas don't mesh well. I want them both, but I want Jesus more. I had to allow God to redefine success for me. As long as I was defining the plan of my life, I would resemble a puppy dog chasing his tail. I would pray and ask Jesus to use me or to help me in a certain situation, but then I'd turn and try to do it all myself.

What does total surrender look like? More importantly, how can I get there? I can want to be surrendered and never actually relinquish control to find my fullest potential, I'm basically asking for an overhaul. I need to lose all the fleshly efforts that make me comfortable and I must rely on something unseen and unknown but purely divine. David Platt, in his book, Radical, says this: "Radical obedience to Christ is not easy... It's not comfort, not health, not wealth, and not prosperity in this world. Radical obedience to Christ risks losing all these things. But in the end, such risk finds its reward in Christ. And he is more than enough for us."

That's a central message to our hospital experience. Learning to trust God and then remembering He can be trusted no matter what – that's something that was forged through this trial. Every day presents me with the opportunity to go my own way and never once consider what God might want. The farther I am away from my wilderness, the easier it is to slip into self-reliance.

You are good and do only good; teach me your decrees.
Psalm 119:68 (NLT)

Encountering Jesus helps me choose to trust again. I want my future to be forever marked by my obedience and His faithfulness. Anything that comes my way can be used by God for good. I love to realize that He is holy, and I know that I need to always see that He is sovereign. But to rely on His goodness makes me heart skip a beat and then rest in His presence. The same emotions I was seeking from my Hollywood ending can be found along the way if I rely on the One who made and loves me.

One of my Uncle Bill's favorite verses is James 1:17 (KJV). I hear him pray it every month at our prayer meetings and I even hear him say it around the dinner table. It reiterates the idea of trusting in God's goodness by saying, "Every good gift and every perfect gift is from above, and cometh down from the Father of lights, with whom is no variableness, neither shadow of turning."

God doesn't change. He doesn't leave. If He is here, then He is doing good. For now, I must be content with struggle and pain and always feeling a little bit short. I must trust that God can redeem absolutely anything I've ever experienced. I will receive my happily ever after, but it will be glory. It will be indescribable, beautiful and perfect and more than I deserve. No fairy tale needed; Prince Charming need not apply. I'm being prepared for something greater than any man could write and I'm trusting in a God that's better than I could ever dream.

Chapter Thirteen

Lesson Eight
Walk Even as Jesus Walked

"Now by this we know that we know Him, if we keep His commandments. He who says, "I know Him," and does not keep His commandments, is a liar, and the truth is not in him. But whoever keeps His word, truly the love of God is perfected in him. By this we know that we are in Him. He who says he abides in Him ought himself also to walk just as He walked."

1 John 2:3-6 (NKJV)

Consistency

I've been told that it's remarkable that I am the same type of person no matter where you meet me. As a leader, daughter, individual, employee or friend; I live by a set of beliefs that mark every aspect of my life. I regard this consistency as one of my greatest characteristics and I really hope that others respect and value it too. We've always said that if you didn't like me in one area or for one reason, then it's likely you're not going to like me in another. I love that I have a set of principles and that they are evident in everything I do.

When faced with the trial's life can throw you, it's good to know how you should respond. Although some people don't always understand this unique quality, I know that there are many circumstances I've endured because I valued stability. I don't always react the way people expect and overcoming disappointment is easier when you have a safe place to land. Since the majority of life is handling success and failure, both gain and loss, there are some things you must have decided before life gets underway.

Through all the experiences, we've been shaped and transformed into who we are supposed to become. By being submitted and surrendered to God, He is redeeming and repurposing all our situations. No matter how we handled everything the first time around, upon learning and changing and growing, we can confidently move forward and be a good kind of different.

We must be different to be better. Even when we struggle or barely keep it together, we astonish those that are watching. I like to surprise people by being stronger and braver and happier than they anticipate. I've learned that acting this way without the heart change is almost impossible and ends up negatively impacting your life, but to be genuine and allow the Spirit to move in the awful times, it's not a masquerade – it's meaningful. After going through our hospital situation, when any type of reaction could've been our instinct, it's so good to know that Jesus was who people saw first.

Being consistent is often underrated. I even think telling someone they're predictable is a compliment! I understand that it's not romantic or glamorous, but it's so refreshing. It's a little frustrating at times when it comes to things like meals and music, but other than that, consistency is entirely worth it.

Evening out the highs and lows that you experience throughout life is a gift and a blessing from God. When the doctors would report good news, we didn't want hope to jump too far to the right... but when they only had negative information to share, we also couldn't jump too far left and settle into depression. It was the consistency our souls found in Christ that helped us remain focused and stable and sure.

Faith is our sure footing when the world around us quakes. Faith will forever mark the person that can sleep through the storm or sing in the rain. To find peace and joy during chaos is a gift given only by the Maker and Ruler of the universe. I am not stable because I have all the answers. I am not unshaken because I am not surprised. Life scares me daily. If I wanted to, I could easily find something to fear daily; there's plenty to fret over. But more importantly than all of that, there's Someone who taught me to not be concerned with what I can do nothing about. My greatest task in every difficult time is to turn both the situation and the care for everyone and everything involved over to Him.

That is why I tell you not to worry about everyday life—whether you have enough food and drink, or enough clothes to wear. Isn't life more than food, and your body more than clothing? Look at the birds. They don't plant or harvest or store food in barns, for your heavenly Father feeds them. And aren't you far more valuable to him than they are? Can all your worries add a single moment to your life? And why worry about your clothing? Look at the lilies of the field and how they grow. They don't work or make their clothing, yet Solomon in all his glory was not dressed as beautifully as they are. And if God cares so wonderfully for wildflowers that are here today and thrown into the fire tomorrow, he will certainly care for you. Why do you have so little faith?

Matthew 6:25-30 (NLT)

Our trust doesn't come from our own efforts, but from our one ability to rely on God. To walk as He walked. Humans have been gifted with the right and ability to choose. In the same breath that I confess negative thoughts, I could've chosen words of life. Our faith that has been nurtured and built over time comes through in the difficult seasons. We don't have time to fret or worry; we must be about a better business. Jesus is as able and ready and willing as ever. If you must forsake all else, be consistent in this one thing: Him.

Junk Heaps and Jesus

One question has haunted several of my difficult seasons. "Who am I?" This inquiry shows no discrimination. Whether you're a man, woman, child, elder, homeless person, or CEO; we can all be confronted with our inadequacies. But when life hurts more than usual, this question seems to pop up often. Even the ring of the words stings more than I am used to. If I strip away what I do, what I think, who I help, the money I make, and the plans I have, then what remains? What good am I if I'm not progressing or performing?

I'm not great at explaining my feelings to others. I know how to hide, and I know how to avoid situations and I have learned how to sugar coat my answers. But living authentically, with sincerity and rigorous honesty, showing grace to myself and others... yeah – I wasn't there yet. In those awkward times, I had to rely on what the Word said was true about me. In all the noise, you can't trust what you feel. It's so important to know the truth, to have people willing to speak the truth into your life and to trust the truth no matter what the days may bring. My internal battle with worthlessness followed me through these bitter seasons. When I reached my limits, the lies got louder and I'm not sure I could've told you who I really was.

I think we all felt lost that summer; I can't even imagine what Mom and Dad went through. They both had such big dreams. I wonder what those dreams looked like from a hospital bed? They knew their mission wasn't complete and that the Lord still had work for them to do. But we all placed such a high value on our work for Jesus that we didn't always see how dedicated He was to His work in us. He didn't bless us because we were so good; He gave us many blessings and He sustained us through many trials just so we could bring Him glory. We strive to serve the Lord well, but each person in my family has been placed in a position where we might never have been able to serve Him at all. And in that scary place, His love didn't waver, His plans weren't changed, and His favor was still free. Jesus was not afraid of our new limitations; in fact, I think He uses us more now because of them.

No one plans for life to fall apart, but when it does (and it will), you must have something on the inside of you that can withstand the pressure. One of the many blessings of being a Christian is that we have Christ in us. (See John 14:17 and Romans 8:9-11) He gives direction and purpose to who we are. Everything we once thought, said, and did should now be under the new authority that abides in our life. But I propose that this is not enough; there must be more. I believe that Christ in us is only the beginning. All the anguish and agony that the world tells us we must go through is not ours to participate in.

I contend that there is a place in our walk with Christ Jesus when, not only is He in us, we are in Him.

As you have therefore received Christ Jesus the Lord, so walk in Him, rooted and built up in Him and established in the faith, as you have been taught, abounding in it with thanksgiving.

Colossians 2:6-7 (KJV)

Let me give an illustration. My family loves to work on old cars, especially the fixer-upper kind. One day, we find an old car that's on its way to the junkyard. Its owner wants to "junk it" and sell it for scrap parts. However, today, it came across our path and we wanted to "save" it. So, after a little haggling, we purchase the piece of junk and bring the car home. From the time we said that we wanted the car, its destination changed. It was no longer headed for the junk heap; it was headed for a home. In spiritual terms, that's Christ in us. We were on the road to destruction, living in a pit of sin and death. However, at the time of our acceptance of Christ Jesus, our destination changed. Now, we are no longer headed for the junk heap; we have an owner, one that wants to make His home with us and care for us.

After buying the car, we bring it home and it sits in our front yard. The ladies cry because they don't really understand, but the men of my family have always been able to see the potential. On the worst days, the Creator can still see what we can become. There is something in my dad and my Pawpaw that cannot let that car just sit there and continue to rot and be worthless. Thus, begins the salvaging process.

Salvaging requires time, talent, and treasury. Never forget that it takes longer to build a house on the rock (Matthew 7); it's always harder to do things the right way. By sanding and scraping, you can remove all the rust. With a little more elbow grease and all the right tools, you can pop out dents, make fenders straight and put lost pieces back where they belong. It's easy to get discouraged; things tend to look worse before they start to look better. But soon, that car begins to take shape. You can see that it will have our "stamp" on it. We've used our favorite colors of paint, our specialty products, and our expertise to make this one of the nicest running machines on the road. This is the part where we are in Christ. As a sinner, when we come to Christ, He refuses to leave us rusted, unwanted, and worldly. One of God's most dominant character traits is that he hates to see His children suffer; He is gracious to a fault. He hates for us to not live in the abundance and in the joy and in the thanksgiving that his death bought. Jesus knows our potential; He sees us for what we can be. When He is in us, we are going to make it to heaven. However, when we are in Him, the life until heaven is more than just worth living, it's enjoyable.

> When Christ is in us, we are going to make it to heaven. When we are in Him, the life until heaven is enjoyable.

If you abide in Me, and My words abide in you, you will ask what you desire, and it shall be done for you. By this My Father is glorified, that you bear much fruit; so, you will be My disciples.

John 15:7-8 (KJV)

How do we get here? Where is the life that is enjoyable? I know I had several miserable years while I was figuring this part out. Every single day of my life is not perfect now that I'm allowing God to work on me. I still have lots of flesh that needs to be crucified daily and I have more questions than ever. I expect many of them to remain unanswered and I'm not even a little sad about that. At every single point, the Lord is making me more like Him. From the inside out, He is overhauling me. There is something oddly satisfying about this being His project and not mine. Having to admit my short comings has made me readier to receive help. Therefore, I have met some awesome people, our ministries have grown, and we are able to reach farther and do more than I ever felt was possible.

There is a place where we can bear "much fruit." It's a life of excellence and abundance. Even in the worst of times, I walked through the valleys with Jesus. I in Him, He in me. This partnership is sure; God's plan is perfect. The discipline that this required has made me a better leader and follower. Even for my parents, our weaknesses became strengths in the salvaging hands of God. All our questions, fears and limitations cause us to rely on God more. When He goes to work, He is an expert in the exceedingly, abundantly and beyond.

What Matters Most

And Jesus answered and said unto her, 'Martha, Martha, thou art careful and troubled about many things: But one thing is needful: and Mary hath chosen that good part, which shall not be taken away from her.

Luke 10:41-42 (KJV)

I'm a Martha, but I've slowly been turning into a Mary because I'm exhausted. My identity is slowly changing, but I think it's due to my ever-increasing awareness of stress levels and limitations. I'm usually the worrier, the planner, the thinker, and a group's voice of reason. I've been careful and troubled about many things. But once you've had an experience that rocks you to your core, and you're willing to analyze and process it, I don't see how you can ever be the same.

Mary was sitting at the feet of Jesus, a place I truly long to be. With parties to plan and people to please, she had only one place on her mind. She could see how important He was above everything else; He had all she would ever need, and He was better than all the other good things she was seeking. Jesus said that one thing is needful. In the end, one thing remains. I don't like to think how close we've come to that end, but I know I've seen the shadows of death, I've heard our cries of desperation and I've felt the hopelessness of pain. We could've started over with anything and I know it would've been easier to give up entirely, but we chose to only rebuild the best.

Dad says that once you experience the extremes of life and death, some things just don't matter anymore. He had to decide what he would continue doing, even if it could kill him. Daily distractions arise, but the heart of the matter doesn't change. There is something inside us, calling for us to stay true to what matters most. Pawpaw would say, "You gotta keep the main thing the main thing." The following is a list of our priorities. It is short, but it still feels complete. After another hundred years, these will still be the most important things we refuse to live without.

JESUS

Not church. Not religious responsibilities. Our new definition of Christianity would know fewer bounds, but our purpose would be more resolute. Some would say stubborn, but I disagree – stubbornness and resolve are not the same thing. We are so sure about a few things. Serving Jesus, becoming more like Jesus, making Jesus known, seeking His face, establishing His kingdom – that's what our worship will be.

When the world fought to make us find something more "normal," we fasted and prayed until Jesus showed us a new and exciting way. Our ministry now is touching hundreds of lives each year, overcoming all types of denominational divisions, providing for the forgotten, caring for the widows and the orphans and seeing people experience Christ in new ways. It doesn't look like any other church in our area, and we are ok with that. Recently, we were able to define our new direction as, "Leading Others to Live and Love Like Jesus." That's been the goal of our ministry all along; a sentence that started being written in 1980 didn't really make a whole lot of sense until now. We wouldn't be here without every single piece of our puzzle, so we are more able to rejoice in every part of the journey now that we see such purpose. Nothing like some big shoes to fill.

But I believe in resemblance. I want my life to resemble Christ's. To do that, I must know Him intimately. I must follow Him closely, and I must change my patterns and behaviors to be more like Him. His strength and His Spirit have residence in my soul, so this really is not a difficult step. He has saved me so many times and He has loved me in my most unlovable state. He deserves my total adoration, my complete attention, my humble appreciation. It matters that I see Him this way. He is the Author of my story, the Finisher of my faith. Although my ministry surprises some people, the fact that He led me here doesn't surprise me at all. When I am picking my priorities, He and His work and His calling are no doubt at the top of my list.

FAMILY

My family is the greatest God-given blessing in my life. After life and death, marriage and babies, I would say that my immediate family currently consists of sixteen people. I'm an only child, but I'm crazy close to my aunts, uncles, and cousins. On any given day, you may find four generations of us around a supper table. We all live within thirteen miles of each other, work together often and still enjoy our life. Even though we go about our daily lives in individual ways, we know that a tight-knit family unit is one of our strongest qualities. My family gives me a safe place to fall. Somewhat like the church, just like a body, we are all small parts of a whole. Each has a role to play; each has a talent or perspective unique from the rest. Everyone knows that we are better together. We are happy to serve each other, knowing that sometimes quality time means helping one move into new houses, sorting clothes for our ministry, trying a new restaurant or driving to a doctor's office. I rely on them and they rely on me. There's a lot of patience required to be this known by fifteen other people, but there's also no fear because the people that know you best love you anyway. I spent a lifetime taking these relationships for granted, but it's impossible to overlook this blessing when you really think about what matters most.

CREATIVITY - ART, MUSIC & CULTURE

Creativity fuels us. This seems like a petty inclusion, especially when all my other priorities are much weightier. However, our passion for the arts is visible and audible and clear. All of us play instruments and we have spent a lot of time playing music together (sometimes we even all play the same song, at the same time, in the same key and tempo). We only sing in church because my great-grandfather, long before I was born, said that we should use our talents and abilities to preach redemption and the cause of Christ. We're country to the core and we can't really help that. But from the songs we write to the old hymns' others can sing along to, there's no denying that music almost courses through our veins.

When Dad was recovering, nothing was going to be right until he could sing and play again. A piece of him was missing. Without being able to get up each morning and play the piano or guitar for Jesus, he was just not himself. The tracheotomy they used to save his vocal chords from a breathing tube had still done some damage to his throat. He could no longer sing in the same key he used to. His muscle memory had been affected, so it took much more effort to play his instruments than it did only six weeks before. And that's just all the technicalities. What about all the emotional changes we had gone through? We were all much more raw; yes, it was authentic too, but sometimes it was just sad. We wanted to sing and say things unlike anything we used to do. Our wilderness experience had changed us all and our music would be forever affected too.

My roots eventually led me to art school. Being able to visually express myself was priceless. Enjoying travel, food and culture inspires me and gives me life. I'm trying to build a life I don't need a vacation from, but I hope to never lose my sense of wonder and adventure. I believe my Creator gave my soul the desire to create. I think Jesus loves when we follow in His footsteps, leaving such beautiful lasting impressions for all the world to see.

You might be surprised to know that this is what matters most to me because my days are packed with plenty of things not on this list. Jobs, friends, hobbies, and entertainment have proven more distracting than some might think. Don't let my facade fool you, sometimes days go by without me ever turning my full attention to prayer or the Word. Writing causes me to focus on Jesus for a little while, but even this journey is just an item on my daily to-do list sometimes.

You see, my calendar is full every day because I thought that's what God wanted. I'm trying to be a faithful laborer, ready for harvest, willing to scream, "Here am I. Send me!" I want to be found waiting and watching, not waiting and wanting. The Bible is full of examples where work was part of the journey, but now I see that the work – the labor, the toil, the pain – may be required from life, but it's always the quiet, the easy and the simple that find Jesus. In the fight against worthlessness, I just add more to my plate to prove my necessity and overcome my insecurities. I have good reasons to be as busy as I am, but the words now seem so hollow. They echo like excuses, making noise but meaning nothing.

the work, labor, toil and pain may be required from life, but it's always the quiet, easy and simple that find Jesus.

All the internal struggle I've uncovered has led me to a better place. All my busyness wasn't going to fix my value. I surrounded myself with some amazing people in a Bible study last year though, and I began to replace the lies I had believed about myself and my worth with true statements from Jesus. Once my ideas concerning my worth changed, then I was able to slow down the pace of my life. I can say "no" to things that don't really apply to me, all without fear of letting others down. I can leave margin in my daily life, knowing that sometimes life happens in wide open spaces. I can filter my passion and my drive through a simple list of my priorities, finding that I'm plenty busy without all my stress and striving.

Generations of people will be blessed because I'm willing to make these tough decisions today. All the seeds we're planting, all the hope we're giving, all the joy we share - who knows the value of such things for all eternity? Identifying the items for my priority list is easier than remembering them, but the difficulties just prove they're worth fighting for. They mark my life in so many evident and unforeseen ways, but I wouldn't change it for the world. The hard times have come and gone, but I would bet that they return. When they do, we'll be ready because we've already chosen what matters most.

Chapter Fourteen

Lesson Nine
Feed. Clothe. Visit. Love.

Then the righteous will answer Him, saying, "Lord, when did we see You hungry and feed You, or thirsty and give You drink? When did we see You a stranger and take You in, or naked and clothe You? Or when did we see You sick, or in prison, and come to You?"

And the King will answer and say to them, "Assuredly, I say to you, inasmuch as you did it to one of the least of these My brethren, you did it to Me."

Matthew 25:37-40 (NKJV)

My Why

Something inside of my heart always knew that God was working behind the scenes. Even when I couldn't feel it or see it, my spirit knew to trust His promises and that our faith would work itself out. That doesn't mean I always knew what to expect, but I at least knew where to turn and to whom I should listen.

While I continually hoped for the best scenario and a total healing for my dad, I can't say that it was always easy. It would be foolish to ignore what the doctors were saying. All the bad news they shared revolved around my father being eternally stunted – having no memories, skills or future. All they could see through the medical tests were problems and all they could offer me were concerns. I still have the packet of papers we declined to fill out that would've approved Dad for permanent disability. They are only partially complete, sitting in a large envelope in a drawer of my office desk. That's another remnant that helps me remember. It's my evidence that our God was bigger than our diagnosis.

When we say that our faith pulled us through, that's only the first part of the story. I know that unpacking the actual events and emotions will help so many others, so I'll see if I can explain what went through my mind. Here's my why.

What helped us get out of bed in the morning? What let us hear the doctors' words and still believe the promises of God? What kept us holding on when all seemed lost?

Is not this the fast that I have chosen? to loose the bands of wickedness, to undo the heavy burdens, and to let the oppressed go free, and that ye break every yoke? Is it not to deal thy bread to the hungry, and that thou bring the poor that are cast out to thy house? when thou seest the naked, that thou cover him; and that thou hide not thyself from thine own flesh?

Then shall thy light break forth as the morning, and thine health shall spring forth speedily: and thy righteousness shall go before thee; the glory of the Lord shall be thy reward.

Then shalt thou call, and the Lord shall answer; thou shalt cry, and he shall say, Here I am. If thou take away from the midst of thee the yoke, the putting forth of the finger, and speaking vanity;

And if thou draw out thy soul to the hungry, and satisfy the afflicted soul; then shall thy light rise in obscurity, and thy darkness be as the noon day:

And the Lord shall guide thee continually, and satisfy thy soul in drought, and make fat thy bones: and thou shalt be like a watered garden, and like a spring of water, whose waters fail not.

And they that shall be of thee shall build the old waste places: thou shalt raise up the foundations of many generations; and thou shalt be called, the repairer of the breach, The restorer of paths to dwell in.

Isaiah 58:6-12 (KJV)

These words were given to my family when they started our church in 1980. When we were figuring out the mission and purpose of our ministry, God specifically directed my parents to

Isaiah 58:12. They didn't have all the answers, but they knew they were undoubtedly called to "raise up the foundations of many generations" and become "the repairer of the breach, the restorer of paths to dwell in."

Our no-longer-small hometown has a history of religiosity. If building churches was all we came to do, we wouldn't succeed. There were people on every corner building churches better than we could. Our task was never the congregation, but the congregant or the parishioner over the parish. We sought out people, individuals, homes, kids, business owners, teachers, and evangelists. We wanted to do life with them and encourage a huge group of Christ followers to peel away the masquerade and live a genuine faith before our community. That involved so much more than singing or teaching; that calling gets messy and we're all a little scarred from being honest and vulnerable in these unsafe environments. However, we wear those scars proudly, trusting fully that God hears and heals.

What if some were unfaithful? Does their faithlessness nullify the faithfulness of God?

Romans 3:3 (NIV)

In the middle of the hospital experience, Mom and I stood on Isaiah 58 because we had not yet seen that full vision come to pass. God couldn't be done. When the Lord gives you a promise, you must also accept that He is the only one that can complete it, but He will see it through.

Even though we had seen more than we'd ever care to and we were struggling with complacency, we still held ALL of God's Word in high regard. God had given His Word and no matter how many humans had disappointed us, God was still perfectly faithful. In His own way, He was right on time. After twenty-five years of ministry, God was redefining our work and reminding us of His plan. We could've never orchestrated these events; frankly, I would've chosen the shorter and easier way. But we all know that God knows best, no matter how uncomfortable or how frustrating reality may currently feel.

After that long summer, we spent a lot of time in the Word. Trying to make sense of it all drove us to our knees more frequently than usual. But when we were seeking answers, God continued to reiterate everything He had previously said. He didn't send new information; He just quietly worked in and through our new situations to remind us that He had only begun.

I wanted new ideas and new directions, but He brought us back to Isaiah 58. This time, we read the whole chapter. When we spent some time in verse 6, we realized that the act of fasting had brought about the results we had been looking for. According to this passage, if we want to see the oppressed set free and a bright light shine forth in gross darkness, we were going to have to fast and pray. The type of fast ordained by God was not one for show or pride, but one of total grace and humility. Our brokenness would be our greatest asset to His team.

Our brokenness would be our greatest asset to God's team.

We began fasting at that point. Dedicating certain times and seasons to God has changed our lives. We felt immediately that we could not hijack the plan of God; if we were looking for the results promised in Scripture, then we would simply follow the rules He provided too. Fasting is still something we feel called to do, and we're as sure today as ever before that it makes all the difference in the world.

If we want to see God transform our lives and communities, then He's going to need to use us. He will be doing all the work, but we will be His earthen vessels. Yes, we feel very out of place and under-qualified. Our mission and purpose as a church, and even sometimes as believers, doesn't necessarily fit the mold that American Christianity has taken on. This is something exciting and difficult and new. As long as there is breath in our lungs, we will continue to tell people the truth of the Gospel and love a community of broken sinners saved by God's grace.

Our wilderness experience tested and tried all that we knew to be true. In the end, we were not unaffected. In many ways, we were confirmed. While many parts of God's plan are identical to the vision He shared more than thirty-five years ago, we are now different people. I dare say that we are now more fully equipped to accomplish His purposes. We've learned to listen, and we are willing to wait. When God asks us to move now, He can trust that we are going with Him and not without His strength and power.

Me Too

Recently, I sat around a circle in a group of twenty-seven women as each poured out their heart to a bunch of strangers. This experience was just step one of a twelve-step program I had been attending. I know I'm not your typical addict, but the process was quite helpful. I started by identifying my own sinful patterns, and boy were there plenty! I then recognized that I'm powerless over sin and Jesus is my only answer. We worked through other truths and really dug deep, dedicating almost a year of our life to becoming better by the time we were done. Done is a technical and shallow term for the conclusion of our group meetings; I will in fact be living my regenerated life for many years to come.

At first, I shied away from participating because my pain just doesn't compare to what some of the other ladies were going through. As they share their stories of addiction and abuse, my formerly self-righteous attitude melts away and I find that I can hold no judgment over these ladies. Only my religiosity lets me differentiate between our sins. My God's holiness sees it all as failure to meet a righteous standard, but He loves me any way. I am no better or worse than any of my peers. I belong in this circle and I'm journeying toward wholeness too.

One of the most powerful truths I've recently uncovered came to me because I survived a wilderness in a hospital and because I was brave enough to navigate my healing with a circle of wonderful women. The greatest pairing of words in the human language is, "Me too."

When we were in the hospital waiting room for more than four weeks, no one had answers that could help us. We did have numerous friends that came to sit for hours on end and we were genuinely cared for by family and strangers alike. No one ever actually came out and expressed their understanding using those words, but their closeness said it all. We were all in this together.

With my recovery group, I'm not supposed to try to fix people. We could talk and discuss and encourage and inform, but that wasn't really the time for advice. Some people cried; some were silent. Other times, we would end a meeting with several angry outbursts, but then even more meetings ended with laughter and praise. It was a crazy journey, an emotional roller coaster, but no matter the ride or the outcome, I'll never forget the times a smile would slip across another's face and you know that they had been there too.

Instead of simply building a church or trying to fix a congregation, I want to climb down in the muck of real life and tell people that I understand. Instead of trying to solve the poverty that's hidden in suburbia, I want to sit at a crowded dinner table in a dirty house and let a vulnerable person know that they are still loved beyond belief. Instead of letting everyone think that I have it all together, I want to be authentic and wear most of my dirt for the world to see. I want to be relatable and respected. I want others to see God's work in me and believe that they are not too far gone. Every time I dare to say, "Me too," I'm letting someone know that they are not alone.

Each of those ideas above is far-fetched if I am unwilling to listen or too scared to speak. Listening is a lost and dying art form. The pauses I use when conversing with others are not just me waiting on my turn to talk. When I am silent, and someone is speaking, I want to let their words resonate deep within my soul. And when I speak, it's not with frivolous filler but every moment should be marked by truth. My responses should be full of care and concern, putting others' needs before my own and finding ways to point people to Christ.

I've learned that when people need you to listen, they

The greatest gift we can give is ourselves.

don't necessarily need you to fix them. It's not your actions that solve the most basic human problem; it's simply your existence. Just knowing that someone has heard them and that their pain or sadness is not unique helps everyone process reality better. The greatest gift we can give is ourselves. Whether we lend an ear or hand, it's our hearts that are moved. In every situation where this holds true, beautiful things take place.

The Word tells us that Jesus was tempted in various ways, but that all of them were common to man (1 Corinthians 10:13). It was so we could say that we have a High Priest and an Intercessor that has been touched with human loss and pain, but that the perfect sinless nature of the Spirit can still prevail (Hebrews 4:15). When I seek God about something that upsets me, His answer can honestly be, "Me too." He is hurt by the lost and dying, the sad and alone. He is hurt by our fear and our lack; He's moved to action by His desire to be present with His people.

In my maturity, I quit trying to fix everyone and I stopped searching for every single possible answer. I'm not ready for anything nowadays and I'm often surprised by what I share with those I might be ministering to. I guess I can't say that I'm never ready, just that I don't pre-prepare. I strive to be vulnerable and authentic, two traits that have never marked my life. We don't minimize or glorify sin and situations; we just take everything one step at a time. I enter circumstances with Jesus eyes and I hope He uses whatever words come out of my mouth to the best of His ability. Most of the time, it will include fewer words than I used to be accustomed to and often, it's as simple as "Me too."

Reach Out

Our church has been meeting at one of the oldest buildings in Frisco since we purchased the old Methodist property in 1982. The sanctuary was built in 1915 and still has pews and stained-glass windows. Our congregation in this century has always been small, so we constantly entertain offers to rent our facilities. Saying that at least two people a week ask to rent, lease or purchase our property would not be an understatement. In March 2009, we met for lunch with one of the newer churches in town; they were looking for a space to meet and were hoping we could help. It didn't take long to figure out that we wouldn't be a good fit to share the same buildings, but that didn't keep us from building good friendships with their leadership team. At one of our meetings, the assistant pastor asked, "Did you know there are kids around here that don't have school supplies?" The short answer was, "Yes;" the longer answer will take a little more time to tell.

I'm the fifth generation of my family to be raised in this town. When I was in elementary school, our city was small yet diverse. There were many different socio-economic factors, all much too big for my young brain to understand. All I knew is that my soccer team had girls with huge homes because they hosted the pool parties, but my team also had some lovely girls that needed a ride from the trailer park to each practice because their mom didn't have a car. For me, Frisco wasn't yet the suburbs and all our residents knew how to get along. As we've grown, neither of those facts remain true.

With a population of now more than 170,000, Frisco feels like its own metropolis. We have the traffic and taxes and tourism that make much larger cities such great places. Nothing against all the growth, it's just not exactly what I signed up for. As the city's borders expanded, the economic diversity didn't grow proportionately. Most residents would now be labeled wealthy, but there always has been and always will be those with less, those that struggle and those in need.

When the local ministry leaders asked if I was aware of the people in need, I said yes and began to quote some of the perspective I just shared with you. At the time, I didn't know more than that. Our church didn't have a history of reaching the community. We always had our doors open and we had regular mission offerings, but this awakening was going to lead to something new.

Our new rag-tag team began to dream about meeting this local school supply need. Some of my evangelist friends knew how to make pancakes by the hundreds, so on a random Saturday in August 2009, we met at our church (because of location) and served breakfast to anyone who wanted to come. That year, we put out four hundred fliers and served almost three hundred people pancakes. We had no clue what we were doing when we started collecting supplies and we ran out long before everyone was seen. We offered to open back up the next Thursday. If we could collect more items, then we would be able to provide more at that time. Surprisingly, many came back to finish their shopping and we felt as if we had accomplished that which we set out to do.

The next month, our leadership team met for coffee with a few people that had volunteered at the giveaway. What I believed to be a one-time thing quickly turned into a vision for more. If local families needed help with school supplies, what in the world were they going to do about all the extra expenditures for Christmas? I don't even recall anyone saying an answer out loud. It was unstated yet understood. We would collect toys and do another event in December 2009 to meet our neighbors' needs again.

We have now been distributing items, loving our neighbors and continually adapting for almost ten years. With more than twenty community events behind us, we still have so much we'd like to do. Here in Frisco, our most impoverished homes share stores, schools and streets with unimaginable luxury. The disparity is almost palatable. Kids from both sides are expected to excel in school while balancing activities, acquiring the latest fashions and pleasing all their friends. It's impossible to keep up. Being employed isn't enough to be happy. Owning all the right things will still leave you falling short. With our bullying, addiction and suicide rates on the rise, the so-called "perfect life" isn't even attainable here. The American dream is a great goal, but it's one that is literally out of reach for the majority of those I get to serve.

Just because we look all right doesn't mean that we are. People who are struggling in the suburbs need to be served differently than those who live on the streets or those experiencing the deeper poverty of third world countries. Here poverty can be spiritual, emotional, psychological and relational as well as monetary or physical. We hope to meet people in that mess, to speak life when no one else speaks at all. Our mission is restoring hope and humanity. By building relationships, we can break the bonds of poverty and help them see that something better exists. They are worth so much more than they have ever been told.

Much of the Bible is open to interpretation. On one hand, there is truth. On the other, we have a few factors that are ever-changing, the assignments just for a season. I am convicted though that we have turned some commands into suggestions. All believers, every church and the entire body of Christ has been called to feed the hungry, clothe the needy and visit the sick and the imprisoned. We are supposed to reach the widows and the orphans. This call is as important as the directive to make disciples. We were born to love others well. The Lord has enabled us to Reach Out to everyone, always. The specifics of that (including our principles, vision and strategies) can be shared at another time. I think the Lord has given that a remarkable story all its own.

Dear friends, since God loved us that much, we surely ought to love each other. No one has ever seen God. But if we love each other, God lives in us, and his love is brought to full expression in us.

1 John 4:11-12 (NLT)

Chapter Fifteen

Lesson Ten
Remember to Not Forget

"And when the Lord your God brings you into the land that he swore to your fathers, to Abraham, to Isaac, and to Jacob, to give you—with great and good cities that you did not build, and houses full of all good things that you did not fill, and cisterns that you did not dig, and vineyards and olive trees that you did not plant—and when you eat and are full, then take care lest you forget the Lord, who brought you out of the land of Egypt, out of the house of slavery."

Deuteronomy 6:10-12 (ESV)

The Purpose of This Pursuit

Let's dig into the Word one more time. When I agreed to recount my life in such detail, being willing to rejoice in the good and rehearse all the bad, I was going to need a pretty good reason.

By faith Jacob, when he was a dying, blessed both the sons of Joseph; and worshipped, leaning upon the top of his staff.
Hebrews 11:21 (KJV)

While running through the hall of faith, I pause now at a small detail I've overlooked for years. In Bible times, men would carve great happenings into their staffs. This helped them keep track of history before tablets and paper were readily available. If they were supposed to teach their children and progeny, how were they to remember?

It's easily believable that Jacob had a staff marked by God's actions in his life. It might've included the promises given to Abraham, the harvests provided to Isaac, the interventions in his own relationship with Esau, and probably even the blessings he would offer to the twelve tribes. This staff was not the reason for his faith; it was the record of it. Jacob worshipped because he remembered.

Let's also remember that his staff likely helped with his limp (Genesis 32:31-32). He leaned upon his staff daily, keeping his record of faith and God's involvement ever before his eyes. This staff was not just a symbol of his faith, an accessory or a piece of his Bedouin uniform. It was a necessity. How often can that be said of my faith? Is it something I tote around for the label or is it there as my stability, my strength and my lifeline?

Forget Me Nots

Studying the Israelites has always been a favorite of mine. We've spoken a lot about their wilderness experience so far, but I'd like to turn my attention to the Promised Land. Walking and waiting have their times and seasons, but so does the blessing and the promise. When the nation of Israel finally crossed the river to inhabit Canaan, God's work was only beginning. Their deliverance started in Egypt, but their relationship with God was literally being walked out daily. One of God's warnings for them was to never forget.

In our introductory passage of Deuteronomy 6, God reminded the children of Israel that they would be living in a land they didn't deserve, drinking from wells they didn't dig and eating from vines and farms they didn't plant. Even their houses would be given to them effortlessly. So, knowing their tendencies (as is the nature of all

> On your good days, rejoice that God brought you here. On the bad ones, rejoice that He hasn't left and He never will.

mankind), God stresses the role of remembering. Remember that you didn't earn this yourself. Remember how good He is and how faithful He can be. Remember every single, little detail and do not forget all the life-altering, gigantic occasions. On your good days, rejoice that He brought you here. On the bad ones, rejoice that He hasn't left, and He never will.

After the summer we had in 2005, I was instructed to never forget. One day, things would get easier and there wouldn't be any darkness in the tunnel. One day, I'd look up and the only pain felt would be in the appearance of the scars. I would eventually get so caught up in something new that I'd be prone to forget the journey that brought me here.

The first anniversary of Dad's heat stroke snuck up on me. I didn't make a calendar reminder and I hadn't been thinking about it, but when I realized how long it had been, I knew I had to commemorate it. Seeing as there were several forty-day fasts in Scripture, I started by fasting from June 23rd to August 1st of each year. At the ten-year mark, the Lord said it was time to change how I remember to not forget. I had spent plenty of time doing without; I needed to finally do something with everything I had learned.

Every wilderness has a purpose. Every pain has a lesson. If we don't remember them, then it might just be a waste of time. I would never be the same after that summer. The call and ministry would never return to what it once had been. All things were new.

We couldn't go back, but we could move on and see what the future could hold.

Our flesh tends to remember all the wrong stuff. The Apostle Paul understood that and wrote in many of his letters to be conscientious about what we remember and what we forget. We should remember that our past is now under the blood and grace of Christ Jesus. We should remember just how wonderful God is to those that love Him; but we should forget the pride, selfishness, vanity and lack that life without Him provides. We should never again dwell on our inabilities, sinfulness and failures.

Like the children of Israel, I have marked my heart. They placed stones in the Jordan River so that every generation had a visual cue. They posted God's promises on their doorways, His law on their hands and on their hearts. I am not the first person God has asked to remember and not forget.

It's not to rehearse the pain. It's not to torture myself. I can't even really hope to make sense of it all. I remember to recall how splendid this walk with God can be, even if it requires a stroll through the valley of the shadow of death. It's to see His handiwork, though my eyes may grow dim. It's to show everyone that it's all about Him and very little about me. It's simply because He asked me to.

Sabbaths and Side Hustles

I'm walking away from this writing experience having learned more than I ever dreamed. This was my story, but I'm still stunned!

Right now, I am trying to adjust to life with a paying job with a non-paying calling. I'm trying to be a good friend, family member, leader and landlord. I'm striving to find balance and I'm losing the battle often. The tendency is to speed things up, add more to the days and hope for better time and team management. Can't everything be solved with a pretty to-do list? No, then maybe a color-coded planner is the missing link?

Experience has proven that my answer is not in a thing or a system or even a process, but it's usually in a Person. Jesus has been the key from the beginning. This story has been more about Him than it has been about me. He is here, helping me wrap this up and teaching me profound truths that I haven't noticed until now.

Everywhere I turn, it seems like the world's answer is hurry. If I look at my occupation as my full-time duty, then everything I do for Jesus would be categorized as a side-hustle. Doing more. Being busier. No room for failure, but also no room for fun. I've bought into this lie for so long that my days can't contain much more excitement. I'm up before the sun, in bed long after everyone else. Admittedly, it's not letting me be happy or healthy. I'm trying to attain a standard I'm not sure really exists. I'm chasing arbitrary achievements, making pointless plans and insisting on daffy deadlines. I could work every day, all day long, and still never feel successful. If hurry is the solution, then I must wonder if it will ever be enough?

I want to slow down during this season each year, finding the time to remember. Even if I'm not fasting, I must fight for the space to never forget. This creates a dilemma. Thank the Lord there is an opposing side of hustle; enter the Sabbath.

And He said to them, "The Sabbath was made for man, and not man for the Sabbath. Therefore the Son of Man is also Lord of the Sabbath."

Mark 2:27-28 (NKJV)

Sabbath. One day each week, given by God to man. Twenty-four hours to do nothing but honor the Lord. Meant to be kept, guarded and revered. We don't have to create our rest, we must enter the rest He has already given us. Maybe it's more about rhythm than it is about balance. Imagine every season having a song – a melody, message, tone and tempo. Fast or slow, simple or full - neither matter when all are in harmony and on purpose.

I want to give the Lord more of my time, all my potential and every bit of my life. I want my calendar to have space for the Sabbath, places reserved for rest and rejuvenation. At the same time though, I don't want to give up the gifts and the callings I feel the Lord has entrusted into my hands. Those projects and organizations and meetings require time and responsibility, but I think they are noble and necessary. My life is going to be loud and busy, but it will have times of silence and sleep. I will go all out, helping and serving and working and dreaming and doing. I will also prioritize recovery and restoration. Jesus will be in both and my calendar will show that I'm seeking both, honoring God in the Sabbath and the side hustle.

Living a Legacy

I feel like my place in history has afforded me a unique opportunity. My Pawpaw is the patriarch of our family and my littlest "nephew" is only six months old. Four generations between them, but we share one family and one calling. Sometimes God asks us to remember things, so we can help other people. I have not forgotten this hospital experience because frankly, I was traumatized by the whole ordeal. But the purpose of my memory goes way beyond that.

I remember things about this wilderness that my parents, grandparents and great grandparents never knew. The kiddos that now fill our family were but figments of our imagination back then. I have kept all these things for my scrapbooks and in my blogs and on my heart. Who is going to be willing to work, to redeem this experience for the glory of God? Who will teach the littles all about the God that led us here? How are they supposed to know how precious they are and how important our story is?

One day, all we'll have is the story and the scars. I still want to leave a legacy, but right now, I'm a little busy living mine.

Conclusion

Dear Jo, summer 2005:

You are in the throws of the darkest time you never foresaw. You don't know if everything will ever be normal again. You are juggling art school and church drama with hospital visits and sick family members. I should go ahead and mention now that it's going to get worse before it gets better. You still don't know who you are or what you're called to be. You feel lost and overwhelmed. I know how hot and still that waiting room is. I can replay June, July and August of 2005 in vibrant Technicolor if you need me to focus on any little detail. I see you and I remember you. You are me. It's in this mess that I need to speak to you.

In a decade, you will still be single, you won't have children and your 401(k) will be non-existent. You will however have the chance to spend a ton of quality time with some beautiful "nephews." Friends will leave gaping holes in your heart, almost lovers will lead you on only to disappoint and you will see many turn away from their best potential, leaving you and Jesus behind to follow other dreams. You'll be confused and sad and lonely at times. You'll also stare in wonder at some of the most beautiful mysteries, moments better than you could ever imagine. You'll find the will to tackle life's greatest questions and you'll become more certain than ever that you were born to change the world.

A lot of that preface just focused on what you will feel and experience in your current season. Now, let's focus for a minute on what you'll still know to be true. After the next ten years of your life, you will know that God is real and that He chases you with an unflinching, unexplainable, matchless love. The works the Lord has for you to do will be undeniable. Giving Him glory will come as naturally as blinking... quick, involuntary and needed. Don't try to keep any of the recognition and don't try to figure out how and why these things will happen. I was once told, "If you try to take the credit, then you'll think you get the blame." Neither is true for your walk with Christ.

Currently, you struggle with your worth quietly but one day, it will be a fight you are more public and humble about. Don't give into the worthlessness and pride now; it's a fight you should start today. You'll encounter a prostitute in New Orleans and she'll make you see your self-righteousness. I'd say that you should deal with that today too, but then we might lose one of the best parts of our story. So, hang tight on that and look for a girl with a guitar in Jackson Square; she'll change your life.

You're never going to have this figured out. Approach it all with curiosity, passion and determination. You feel grown at your twenty years of age and your soul is wiser than you know, but you haven't yet begun to live. As for your calling, you feel like you need more answers, but all you really need is faith. When someone mentions that kids need school supplies and Christmas toys, silence every negative thought and jump in with both feet. It's the biggest and best decision you'll make and after several long years, you won't regret it. As you grow and learn and change, your faith and your family will be your only constants. Lean into both when things are hard, and don't give up on either when you think you can handle it on your own. When you want to stop, keep moving. When you think you've arrived, press deeper.

Pray. Go and sit at the feet of the women who raised you and listen to every word they send up to Jesus. Build your happiness from within. Trust people even when they don't deserve it. Ask the Lord for a testimony, write it down and tell it to anyone who cares. Be tough but not hard. Be graceful but not soft. Leave every place better than you found it. You've been given a good, clean, respectable name – it will open more doors than you'll ever deserve, but you can ruin it all in one fleeting moment. Continue to be amazed at God's favor and follow Him at all costs; your comfort level is an enemy to your dreams.

One of the things you'll realize soon is that you love to travel. You've only been a few places until now, but your twenties will be filled with awesome adventures. Here are some things I wish I had known a little earlier in life:

- It snows a lot in Montana and tire chains are still VERY recommended in early March.
- Driving the PCH in a BMW is worth getting carsick.

- Listen to the GPS and pack plenty of Twizzlers to sustain you through Chicago's traffic.
- Eat local. Hawaii's shrimp trucks, Brooklyn's pizza, New Mexico's green chiles, Atlanta's hot dogs, fried pickles in Memphis and Kansas City BBQ. Try it all.
- Find a band and follow them, literally. Go see them in Memphis, Omaha, Oklahoma City, Stillwater, Gruene, Dallas and College Station.
- You'll visit a few cities multiple times and they will somehow start to feel like home. Go ahead and let this happen; it makes you a better person in the long run.
- Just go to sleep on the wet bus ride from NYC to DC. Also, the museums in both cities need about five times as much attention as you'll plan to give them.
- Stop letting your fears hold you back. Be wise but don't be boring.

Some last bits of wisdom that you'll glean along the way are meant to transform your perspective on the world. Before I get back to living my current life, I'll leave you with this:

- Some of the best things in life don't have labels.
- The battle for your heart is fought on the pages of your calendar. (Thanks, Bob Goff.)
- You deserve the love you keep trying to give everyone else.
- Jesus has grace for the good girl too. (That's Emily P. Freeman.)
- You don't need a reason to help people.

- Never give up on something that sets your soul on fire.
- God is most glorified in you when you are most satisfied in Him. (I'm glad Jeff Deyo likes John Piper too.)
- Stop apologizing for who you are and what you feel.
- Not to spoil the ending for you, but everything is going to be ok.

I'm sorry, for I see now that this is a lot to process. In the end, you can't stop the journey you're on and I pray that you never want to. You will be happy, but you don't really want to feel too satisfied or complete on this side of heaven. You won't recognize where you'll end up, but you'll know it's where you belong. You won't even be able to imagine a life any better. Continually joining Jesus on an adventure is the greatest invitation of all time! You will be forever marked by everything that's happening in your life right now. You might cry when you write to your younger self because the memories are a lot to handle. But you'll see, in time, that this life you lead is worth it. Bear these stories and all the scars proudly.

Never forget that the best is yet to come.

Sincerely,
Jo, circa 2019

Jo Elaine Hooper

HONOR   HERITAGE   HOSPITALITY   HUMILITY   HUMANITY   HOPE

joelainehooper.com

46982572R00115

Made in the USA
Middletown, DE
04 June 2019